Praise for TH[illegible]

T0102137

"Once in a while a book comes along [illegible]*ay you think and act for the better.* The Anxiety Audit *joins this club. I challenge you to put it down and not move through your day differently. Buy this book—it will guide you along the journey to being the person in relationships, and inside yourself, that you are hoping to become."*

—**Rachel Simmons,** bestselling author of
Odd Girl Out and *Enough As She Is*

"Today's uncertain world has created an anxiety epidemic! The Anxiety Audit *shows us how not to let it get a grip on our lives. Lynn Lyons's down-to-earth advice provides simple solutions to help us recognize what's making it worse, what makes it better, and how to manage our hectic lives and our important relationships. I guarantee you'll have page after page of ah-ha moments."*

—**Joan Lunden,** journalist and bestselling author

"Lynn Lyons is an expert in the anxiety field and a skilled therapist, but she talks about anxiety like the rest of us. The Anxiety Audit *is a book full of stories, advice, and humor that will help us get through our busy days, manage our unpredictable world, and improve our most important relationships. Lynn shows us anxiety is part of being human, but it need not define us."*

—**Laura Morton,** *New York Times* bestselling author,
creator of Anxious Nation

"In The Anxiety Audit, *Lynn Lyons writes with clarity, wisdom, and wit. She offers illuminating case examples and practical advice in a sensible, straightforward way. In so doing she provides you with a means of attaining both relief and inspiration. Lynn makes it clear that the goal isn't to cure anxiety. Rather, the far more realistic goal is to learn to manage it skillfully using the insights and strategies she so clearly provides in this wonderful book. Read it, enjoy it, learn from it, and discover for yourself how this audit can yield substantial personal profits!"*

—**Michael D. Yapko, PhD,** clinical psychologist,
author of *Breaking the Patterns of Depression*
and *Depression is Contagious*

"Here is the best gift of The Anxiety Audit: *You won't get bogged down in all the little details of change. You can trust that Lynn knows—she knows!—the seven simple shifts in your perspective that release you from anxiety's grip. Oh, and all that sage advice you've heard through your life? She debunks it."*

—**Reid Wilson, PhD,** founder, anxieties.com

THE ANXIETY AUDIT

THE ANXIETY AUDIT

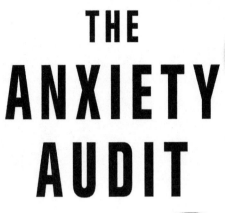

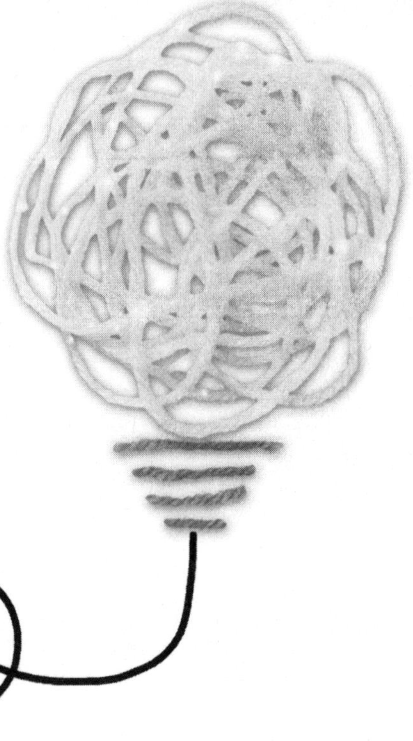

7 Sneaky Ways Anxiety Takes Hold and How to Escape Them

Lynn Lyons, LICSW, coauthor *Anxious Kids, Anxious Parents*

Health Communications, Inc.
Boca Raton, Florida
www.hcibooks.com

Disclaimer: The content of this book is for informational purposes only and is not intended to diagnose, treat, cure, or prevent any condition or disease. You understand that this book is not intended as a substitute for consultation with a licensed practitioner. The use of this book implies your acceptance of this disclaimer. The information presented here does not take the place of advice from your mental healthcare professional or medical healthcare provider. Please seek advice from your healthcare provider or doctor for your particular health concerns.

Library of Congress Cataloging-in-Publication Data
is available through the Library of Congress

© 2023 Lynn Lyons

ISBN-13: 978-07573-2425-3 (Paperback)
ISBN-10: 07573-2425-8 (Paperback)
ISBN-13: 978-075732-426-0 (ePub)
ISBN-10: 07573-2426-6 (ePub)

All rights reserved. Printed in the United States of America. No part of this publication may be reproduced, stored in a retrieval system, or transmitted in any form or by any means, electronic, mechanical, photocopying, recording, or otherwise, without the written permission of the publisher.

HCI, its logos, and marks are trademarks of Health Communications, Inc.

Publisher: Health Communications, Inc.
301 Crawford Blvd., Suite 200
Boca Raton, FL 33432-1653

Cover and interior design and formatting by Larissa Hise Henoch

For Zed, Brackett, Brice, Cole, Pearl, Greta, Kate, and Thomas
May this next generation fill their lives to the
brim with messy, joyful connection.

And for Michael Yapko, who has shaped who I am as a clinician
and whose influence is on every page of this book.

CONTENTS

FOREWORD

A game-changer. That is how people describe the tips and tools that Lynn Lyons gives to those who struggle with any type of anxiety. And I should know. Because she changed my game as a parent and a person.

In the early days of the pandemic, most of us were stuck at home. In the midst of the stress and everyday struggles, many tried to look on the bright side, noting how lucky they were to have a professional chef or baker as a family member. I was fortunate to have an anxiety expert at my disposal—Lynn Lyons, an esteemed psychotherapist, mom, and educator who happens to be my sister-in-law (as well as my doula during the birth of my children).

Lynn and I noticed an uptick in anxiety from the pandemic—waves and waves of uncertainty cresting upon an already-rising tide of anxiety in our society. We decided to launch a podcast called *Flusterclux* to share Lynn's advice and tools with as many families as possible.

Over the years, Lynn has shared life-changing wisdom with professionals and families in her keynotes and workshops as well as with me at our kitchen table. She has taught me what I should be focusing on as a parent to be on the offensive against anxiety before it arises. At the time, I didn't realize I had a very simplistic understanding of her work in terms of how she helps families with anxious children.

In the process of making our podcast episodes, I've learned invaluable skills from Lynn that I didn't know I needed. That's what people say frequently about her work. You may think you know what anxiety is at the start of this book, but Lynn will show you ways anxiety drives your and your family's behavior, casting a much wider net than you realize. Understanding how to identify anxiety's hiding places feels like a magic decoder of human behavior.

The Anxiety Audit breaks down these common patterns. And Lynn unpacks each one of them with as much humor and as little psychobabble as possible. These patterns are everywhere. Learn and identify them so that you can recognize when you are engaging in them, your family does them, or your colleagues do them. Believe me, you will have no shortage of practice.

As you become familiar with your anxious patterns, that's where the magic begins.

Lynn outlines a better way to respond. She coaches you how to interrupt them. With practice it gets easier and easier.

My pattern, for example, is "catastrophizing." Armed with this new information about myself, I can see the changes I have made. As a catastrophizer, anxiety frequently runs a worst-case-scenario movie in my head.

With practice, I began to think to myself, *Oh my gosh! Don't panic, this is just you catastrophizing!* In time, I began to greet my pattern without emotion or judgment. *Hello, anxiety movie. I see you.* And finally, I've learned to hit pause on the anxiety movie from playing and simply say, *Anxiety, I am so bored by your predictable movies. Not today.*

But here's the kicker: Lynn explains why eliminating anxiety is not the goal. You're never going stop being anxious any more than you will stop being angry or sad. So managing our responses is the strongest way to prevent anxiety from controlling our homes. And, conveniently, these skills of managing our emotional responses have broader applications. The work you put into anxiety will reward you with other tricky feelings, too.

You may already think you know your relationship with anxiety, but Lynn explains it in a different way. Anxiety is a big-umbrella term for so many emotions. Be open to new understanding that brings light to the parts of you that you like to keep in the dark. In this book, you will see how universal these struggles are. Take comfort in the fact that everyone is juggling them too.

Every conversation you have while being anxious makes you less capable of authentic connection. Shifting away from anxiety makes room for deeper connection. The results are powerful and nourishing.

This work is life-long. If one only had to read or hear or practice this information once, I would no longer have any anxiety, nor would anyone else in Lynn's family. Nor would Lynn, for that matter. It's ongoing and worthwhile work, especially if you tackle it as a family, out in the open, in the light. Everyone wins.

—**Robin Hutson,** cohost, *Flusterclux*

INTRODUCTION

I share stories. I use them in my sessions with families and when I'm speaking and training. I subject my family to them. They were a huge part of parenting when my boys were little. This book is full of stories: stories about the people I have worked with in my thirty years as a therapist, stories about my own experiences with worry and anxiety because they are just like *your* stories about worry and anxiety, and stories I have collected from here and there because other people's words and tales often convey what I want to convey, only better.

So I start this book with three stories.

The first happened in 1993. I was a newly licensed social worker with a job as a therapist in a small mental health agency. That spring, I headed off with a few colleagues to a huge psychotherapy conference. Over several days, there were at least 100 workshops to choose from: depression, personality disorders, trauma; art therapy, play therapy, sound therapy, sex therapy. It was thrilling at first, but as I went from workshop to workshop, I felt dumber and dumber. I didn't know the terms they were using or the approaches they were discussing. How could I ever learn all these different diagnostic categories? Why hadn't

I learned any of this stuff in graduate school? What language were these experts even speaking? I knew nothing! I left feeling intimidated and overwhelmed.

The second story happened fifteen years earlier in a middle school in 1978. I was a seventh grader at Webb Junior High School, sitting in a classroom doing the required standardized testing with my peers. If we finished early, we were told to take out a book and read. I brought with me Michael Crichton's 1969 novel, *The Andromeda Strain*. I don't remember much about the book, but I do remember that I came across a passage that vividly described someone breaking their nose. I am a squeamish fainter from a family of fainters. Broken bones can undo me. As I read the words about the nose cracking and blood flowing, my ears began to ring. I felt hot and nauseous. Without saying much, I got out of my seat and hurried to the bathroom, my vision closing in. I knew to get down, to preempt the fall. When I regained consciousness, my cheek was resting on the cool tile of the bathroom floor. It felt good. I waited there for a few minutes and then returned, shaky and pale, to my classroom. I said nothing. I knew what triggered this—it was not unfamiliar—but I knew little else. I was glad no one found me, that I'd managed to get through this episode undetected.

I would not learn the term *vasovagal syncope* until decades later, the phrase used to describe this type of fainting that results from a dramatic drop in blood pressure, often caused by the sight of blood or other injuries. I knew my father and siblings did the same thing, but we didn't know what to do about it. We were often ambushed by our imaginations and our reactions if we couldn't successfully avoid the triggers. I'm much better now. Not perfect. I've fainted three times in the last twenty-three years. But back then and well into my late twenties, it was an embarrassing secret. And I was defenseless.

The third story is from 2018. I was at the movies with my parents, watching the newly released documentary on Fred Rogers, *Won't You Be My Neighbor?* I was transfixed. Mister Rogers was my childhood companion, my explainer of the unexplainable. As an adult watching, I was in awe of what he was able to do, how he understood children and the way he gently and consistently challenged the adults. At the end of the film, there is a clip of Mister Rogers giving a commencement speech. And as he often did when ending a speech, he asked his audience to spend a full minute silently honoring those that "smiled us into smiling, walked us into walking . . . loved us into loving."

"Let's just take some time to think about those extra-special people," he said. I began to cry. Not little tears, but full-on, impossible-to-stifle sobs. Sitting there between my parents, my heart opened wide in a way that felt so young and unstoppable, the way you cry when you're a child. I first began hearing his voice and those messages when I was *three years old*, but apparently I missed them. And him. It felt so powerful to hear that language of connection. In 2018 our world already felt tough, angry, fractured. Boy, we had no idea.

These three stories encapsulate why I wrote this book, what I want you to understand about anxiety and worry and stress. It comes down to three words illustrated by the stories I shared. Let me explain.

WORD ONE: SIMPLIFY

The first story is a warning about complicating what needn't be complicated. Anxiety is not complex, but it thrives when we make it so. I know this now, and I want you to know it too. Thirty years after that overwhelming weekend at the conference, my rookie intimidation has been replaced by a recognition (and frequent annoyance, I'll admit) that the mental health field is unnecessarily tangled. And like every other field, it has its trends and lingo and allegiances and creativity and competitiveness. This, of course, can be good and bad. I've seen many a new diagnosis or treatment arrive on the scene cloaked in big promises and legitimate hopefulness. Some have changed in remarkable ways how we understand human beings—for example, the impact of childhood trauma. Others have been discarded or simply faded away. Some have done harm. I firmly believe that complicating anxiety has led to harm. The more I study and observe and experience this anxiety thing, the simpler it becomes. Unlike in 1993, I no longer feel the need to navigate the moving targets of the mental health field. Instead, I work to pull my clients out of that confusing muddle.

The primary aim of this book is to offer a less pathological experience and explanation of anxiety and worry, to rethink the crisis-based, complicated diagnostic labeling that is now so prevalent but is not working. The goal is to simplify. I'll explain how the anxious patterns we learn and practice every day add up over time to make your life predictably more difficult. I'll tell you about the adjustments you can begin to make. Hard work? Perhaps. But not complicated.

WORD TWO: DEMYSTIFY

Anxiety may not be complicated, but it is powerful. Having spent time unconscious on bathroom floors (and many other floors) I offer my testimony: worry and anxiety can literally take you out, in big and small ways. My fainting story illustrates how a lack of understanding keeps us trapped, scared, and overreactive. For most of us, anxiety is not a disorder and doesn't need to be viewed as such, but it's going to show up at some point. It's a common and normal part of being a human. And yet so many of us don't have accurate or helpful information about its patterns and tricks, or even the why and how of the physical symptoms it creates. Anxiety is sneaky. It likes to promote things that are *not* emergencies into emergencies. That's the very nature of its power. Without information or a basic understanding of what's happening and what makes it worse, we begin to worry about our worry. We get anxious about feeling anxious. The natural desire to get rid of our anxiety often leads to choices, internal dialogues, or instructions (from friends, family, and yes, even therapists) that make us feel worse. What we do to stop feeling anxious actually makes us more anxious. I call this spiral "doing the disorder." What we want to do instead is demystify.

The second aim of this book is to pull the curtain back on this anxiety thing and stop that spiral. I want to replace, "What is happening to me?" with, "Oh, I know this pattern." When I finally learned the ins and outs of my squeamish fainting (the vasovagal syncope), I felt like a superhero. I needed this information, but for years I didn't even know it existed. I still faint occasionally, but now when the symptoms show up, I know what's happening and I can (almost always) interrupt the pattern and pull out of the tailspin. I'm no longer doing the disorder. Information demystifies how anxiety works and changes how we respond to it.

WORD THREE: CONNECT

Finally, anxiety disconnects us. It does not care if we see those we love, do what we enjoy, or offer our talents to the world in meaningful ways. It wants us to avoid because avoidance provides immediate relief. It seeks safety and comfort and certainty. Anxiety disrupts our relationships because it is rigid and demands control, and because relationships are messy and sticky and emotional. Anxiety gets in the way of connection because when it makes us feel judged and uncertain and incapable, we take our shame and retreat. Sitting in that movie theater in 2018, Mister Rogers reminded me of the value of connection. Now, after all we've been through, I think we need connection above all else.

Although the bane of loneliness did not arrive with Covid-19, the pandemic amplified the devastating impact of isolation. For many, the past several years have been divisive and lonely, to put it mildly. I have dedicated in this book an entire chapter to the pattern of inner isolation, but the stories of how anxious patterns disconnect us from our loved ones, our lives, and even ourselves are woven throughout. Separation and disconnection feed anxiety and depression. They pull us inside ourselves. My final aim is to convince you—with stories and strategies and usable, concrete steps—that you are not alone. In the words of Fred Rogers, "I think everyone longs to be loved and longs to know that they are lovable."

We're going to simplify and demystify anxiety to make room for connection.

CHAPTER ONE

THE BRAIN HAS NO OFF SWITCH

Sneaky Pattern: How Repetitive Negative Thinking Disguises Itself as Problem Solving

Not causing harm requires staying awake. Part of being awake is slowing down enough to notice what we say and do. The more we witness our emotional chain reactions and understand how they work, the easier it is to refrain. It becomes a way of life to stay awake, slow down, and notice.

—Pema Chodron, *When Things Fall Apart: Heart Advice for Difficult Times*

Many years ago, a spunky ten-year-old named Alex sat in my office and announced, “If we had time machines, you wouldn’t have a job.” He went on to explain that worried kids like him could hop in the machine, zip ahead to see how everything turned out, and then come back to the present, free of the uncertainty that keeps worry going.

"And we could go back in time and rearrange things, too, so we wouldn't have to keep thinking about our screwups. We wouldn't need you."

"Brilliant and likely accurate," I told him. "But since we don't have time machines, I still have a job." And I reminded him that my job was to teach him how to manage the time machine inside his brain, that busy, creative brain that wants to fly into the future to find certainty and obsessively replay the past to find answers and explanations.

Alex was unusually articulate, but his anxious patterns were not at all unique. Virtually everyone I see for anxiety and depression, no matter how young or old, has some awareness that they think too much. "I can't turn my brain off," they say. Or, "I wish I could move past it, but I can't." And sometimes the seductive thought comes, "If I just think about it more, I'll be able to solve the problem."

So, as we begin this anxiety audit, the patterns of ruminating and worrying earn top billing. Why? Because, as Alex explained, our powerful human brains enable us to fearfully imagine things that haven't happened yet—also called *worrying*—and doggedly review things that have already occurred—referred to as *ruminating*. Whether we want to or not, we internally time travel, zipping between past and present and future. It's a common and often useful quest, but far less useful when we try to obsessively think our way into certainty about the future or ponder our way out of past regrets. We imagine the what-ifs and endlessly weigh our options, real or imagined. We project and predict. And we go back, too, retracing the old ground of "if only," replaying conversations and decisions, wishing for a do-over.

What if I mess that up?

What if something horrible happens?

If only I had that comeback ready when I needed it!

If only I'd made a different choice instead.

Why didn't I pay attention to those warning signs?

If we just had more information, more time to plan, another opportunity to try again, we could prevent things and fix things. And life would be manageable, smoother, less *painful.*

Unfortunately, and perhaps not surprisingly, neither of these patterns offer the payoff we wish for or expect. In fact, ruminating and worry, closely related to each other and often referred to together as repetitive negative thinking (RNT), are significant risk factors for anxiety and depression. When researchers examine the pathways into the different anxiety and mood disorders, repetitive negative thinking is everywhere.

The distinction between worrying and ruminating lies in the direction in which the negative thoughts head, with ruminating focusing on the past and worry fretting about the future. You might have a proclivity toward one or the other, while other people are switch-hitters, so to speak. In my experience, people most often do both, but there are some "pure" ruminators out there. Whether I'm referring to ruminating or worry, much of what I describe applies to both patterns.

CHEWING YOUR MENTAL CUD

To *ruminate* literally means to chew your cud. Goats, sheep, cattle, and deer are all in a family called *ruminants,* which means they pull up partially digested food from the first chamber of their stomach (the rumen) and chew on it. And chew on it. While this practice is helpful to a goat's digestion of roughage, it's not so helpful to your emotional, social, and occupational well-being. I often say that ruminating is to productivity what chewing gum is to eating vegetables. When chewing gum, it looks like you're eating. There's jaw movement, teeth action, swallowing, even some flavor, but no nutritional value. Ruminators are looking for some insight into events that have already happened or an alternative way to perceive something they can't change. *If I can think more*, they reason, *I will unlock a new understanding or uncover some detail that was overlooked.* But this mental gum chewing doesn't offer you much. Ruminators tend to focus on loss and regret. They are prone to self-blame and self-criticism, and at times increased judgment of others.

Worrying involves that same repetitive chewing, but the focus is geared toward finding certainty and eliminating discomfort as you look ahead. Worriers time travel into the future and create a narrative based on what might happen. They get locked into what-if thinking and watch their own frightening internal movies about the future. The plot revolves around some horrible thing (*What if my child is taken?*) or something they find overwhelming and believe they can't handle (*What if I screw up my presentation?*). They imagine the scenario and feel anxious, then worry more as a way to find a solution.

Worriers may look fine on the outside, doing what needs to be done and functioning at high levels. Maybe the worrier is busy and accomplished, but those in close proximity know the amount of energy spent on RNT. In more severe cases, worry can interfere with functioning because the worrier strives to rearrange the world to prevent the bad outcome they've imagined. Or, they work to avoid a situation or trigger altogether.

All brains do this to some extent, but some brains are trapped in this type of thinking more than others. Sticky brain (it's really called that) seems to be heritable or genetically passed down, like temperament. When characteristics like sticky brain run in families, you likely get the double combination of the genetic predisposition *and* the powerful family modeling. Heritable does not mean unchangeable, however, and it doesn't mean that it defines you or will take control of your life. As with everything from exercise to ice cream, the quality and quantity of your ruminating and worrying matter. How much overall time you spend with your RNT, how you react to the thoughts when they show up, and the value you place on the thoughts are what make the difference. Let's talk about the dos and don'ts of RNT, and how people unknowingly keep themselves mired in their sticky thinking.

HOW WE STAY STUCK

First, people stay stuck by trying to get rid of their annoying, persistent negative thoughts. "What's wrong with that?" you ask. Getting rid of these annoying thoughts sounds reasonable, doesn't it? Unfortunately, such attempts backfire. I know from talking to thousands of ruminators and worriers that though the goal quite simply is to feel better, the result is almost always the opposite.

This statement is key, so read it a few times: *attempts to get rid of your repetitive negative thoughts paradoxically make them stronger.* This may sound backward and even go against what others have told you, but to lessen the grip of an RNT habit, you must first stop battling it. Trying to eliminate the thoughts and the discomfort they cause is instinctive, but our brains don't cooperate when we tell it to not think about something. If *right now* I asked you to *not think* under any circumstances about a green giraffe or the status of your left big toe, your attention would go there immediately. Before you have a chance to *not go there*, you're there.

Next—and this one makes it even trickier—your mind can get caught in an internal battle about the merits or necessity of such thoughts. It's as if there are two parts of you: one that knows you're ruminating and another that believes (or hopes) that the constant thinking will result in a new perspective or different solution. You're trying to eliminate these annoying thoughts, recognizing them (mostly, kinda, sorta) as problematic but simultaneously *feeling* that the ruminating is somehow helpful and necessary. When you remain trapped in the thinking (and then the thinking about the thinking and trying to get rid of the thinking), self-criticism and frustration thrive. It's a mental hamster wheel. Round and round you go.

Finally, repetitive negative thinkers stay stuck because they believe that going over what has already happened or what might happen will teach them something valuable. This type of thinking, both ruminating and worrying, stays powerful because it disguises itself as problem solving.

It is not.

How many of us have had an encounter with somebody and then later think, *Oh, I should have said that! If only I'd had that response!* Or perhaps you made a mistake, forgot an appointment, or sent the wrong text to the wrong person. Maybe you're trying to decide which appliance to buy, considering a job switch, or fretting about how to hire the best babysitter. When we're in this mode, our brains are busy, but the reality is that sticky thinking does not promote problem solving and is emotionally exhausting. Your mind works internally but resists letting go and moving forward. It's the equivalent of sitting in your car and pressing the brake and gas pedals at the same time. As you mentally go over and over the same ground, your mood tanks, and your stress level rises. You're often disconnected from past lessons learned and your own competence. Self-compassion is in short supply. Somehow, however, you convince yourself that rumination is necessary. It's like an itch you want to scratch.

Groundbreaking and prolific researcher Susan Nolen-Hoeksema spent much of her career looking at the characteristics of ruminators and what they actually *do* when faced with problems. She was one of the first to illuminate the connection between rumination and depression, particularly the impact of this connection on women. Dr. Nolen-Hoeksema (and the many students who expanded upon her work after her death) found that ruminators are passive in nature and often avoidant. Moreover, repetitive negative thinkers are less likely to implement a viable solution that could truly help improve a situation. Despite all that cognitive gum chewing, ruminating ultimately impairs problem solving and negatively impacts motivation.

Ponder that little counterintuitive nugget of information. If you are a ruminator or a worrier, you believe that thinking is the solution or will lead to one. But you are less likely to act on a solution if your friend or your partner or your therapist—or even your RNT—should ultimately offer you one! Stuff doesn't get done.

RUMINATING AND RELATIONSHIPS: A WEDDING, A DIVORCE, A BABY

About twenty years ago, I attended a wedding and sat for a time at a big round table next to Joyce, a woman in her early fifties. We struck up a conversation, wading into the small-talk topics of our connection to the wedding. Joyce and the bride's mother were close friends. Her children were grown, all out of the nest. She was divorced, she said. Her ex had an affair (one of many) and left her for his mistress. She was devastated, she said. I nodded politely as she continued to replay the details of her divorce, the anger she felt, the conflicts they had. Lawyers. Alimony. Comebacks she wished she'd said when she ran into her young replacement. Revenge fantasies that she never had the nerve to pull off. If only she knew then what she knew now, Joyce told me repeatedly, as she reworked the details of her pain.

While some of the exact details are sketchy twenty years later, I clearly remember feeling trapped in the conversation. But how could I interrupt? Her emotions were so jagged and raw. And she seemed to be sitting alone. *I could listen and empathize*, I told myself. *I could be kind.*

Finally, I asked, "Is your divorce final yet?" Joyce snorted. "Of course, dear! He left me seventeen years ago!" I felt something inside me shift.

How many times had she told that story, chewing on the roughage of her heartbreak to whomever would listen? I heard personal, agonizing details, and I was a stranger at a wedding reception! The number of retellings most certainly paled in comparison to the hours she spent ruminating internally. If I felt trapped, can you imagine what it was like for her? And for those who shared her postdivorce life? Had family members pushed her to move on? To date again? Were there eye rolls or avoidance or arguments? I'm sure patience ran low. If I saw her at another event, I'd feel empathy—but honestly, I'd avoid her. I would! She suffered with her sticky thinking, which likely pushed people away. The impact of RNT on relationships is substantial.

Joyce is a dramatic example because her ruminating was so quickly and vehemently expressed. She was stunningly stuck on this single, long-ago event. But run-of-the-mill, day-to-day ruminating will happen to all of us at some point in our lives. RNT bounces around in the ordinary events of our everyday lives, and it absolutely shows up when life goes wrong. The dramatic patterns of RNT may be indicative of an anxiety disorder and, as mentioned earlier, are often a path into depression. They need attention. But recognizing and changing these everyday patterns—patterns that don't meet the criteria of "diagnosable"—is also critical because even low-grade RNT impacts relationships.

When we are ruminating or worrying, we tend to be overly engaged with our feelings and thoughts and less engaged with those around us. This is referred to as an *internal focus* because we turn our attention inward, creating stories. For example, if you tend to be introverted or a bit insecure socially (very common!), you are less externally focused on the other person while you interact with them. Instead, you are editing yourself before you speak, wondering if you said the wrong thing, or even anticipating what you'll do in the next four minutes if you run out of things to say.

After the interaction, you likely analyze the conversation and your screw-ups. As you seek certainty in your fog of doubt, replaying your and their words, expressions, and reactions, you create a one-sided narrative. While some ruminators may argue, "But I'm really focused on the other person when I'm having [or reviewing] our conversations!" the focus is squarely on one's own feelings, thoughts, and perceptions.

PLEASE PASS THE STICKY THOUGHTS

Remember that sticky thinking is both a heritable trait and socially modeled, so the combination of nature plus nurture makes such thinking predictably generational. If you recognize yourself as a ruminator or a worrier, this sticky thinking is probably a pattern in your family of origin. We know anxiety runs in families. Anxious parents are six to seven times more likely to create an anxious child. But we miss the point if we overemphasize genes and neglect the power of modeling.

Anxious families have some predictable dynamics. Anxious parents inadvertently demonstrate how to worry and overthink, both directly with their children and through their own behavior. These parents are less skilled at showing their children how to tolerate uncertainty, independently problem solve, or develop an early sense of autonomy. As a therapist, I frequently see these skill gaps in anxious children.

If raised by worriers, kids also perceive the world as a more dangerous place compared to kids not raised by worriers. My goal with families and schools is to interrupt these generational patterns of RNT and debunk the myth of their effectiveness. Problem solving is active and often collaborative. RNT is passive, internal, and isolating. Once people recognize the impact of these RNT traditions on their own family, it often inspires them to interrupt their patterns going forward.

This was the case with Brittany, a self-described worrier who focused on what might happen in the future and worked hard internally to think and plan her way into certainty. As a new mother, her need to "be sure" felt more intense than ever, and she predictably relied on what she was taught in her family about finding certainty and eliminating all risk—but it wasn't working. Applying this pattern to parenting a newborn soon became exhausting, which is why Brittany sought me out for help.

"I come from a 'processing' family," Brittany told me. "I was taught to think it through, talk it through. We valued intellect. There was a solution there if you just thought hard enough and long enough." She recognized quickly that her mother was a repetitive negative thinker who had a very hard time letting go of past hurts or grudges and would also go over (and over) the details of anything upcoming. Before a family trip or even the first day of school, her mother reviewed lists and asked questions repeatedly. "Are you sure you remembered to pack enough socks?" or "What do we know about the teacher? What have you heard?"

Brittany told me of the unspoken but omnipresent family motto: *Bad things happen, but not if we plan ahead.* I wondered out loud if the family value of "intellect" more aptly described a need for certainty. Sometimes bargain-basement worry likes to dress itself up in more sophisticated language, I said. The demystifying had begun.

Arguments with her husband increased, too. He became frustrated with Brittany's need to control every aspect of their baby's care. "I accuse my husband of being careless because he wants to go do things as a family, just head out and enjoy the day. But I can get so caught up in the thinking and planning and what-if'ing that I won't make a decision or get much done," she told me.

She also recognized that she wasn't truly present with her new baby or her husband because she was reviewing what questions she needed to ask at her baby's next wellness check or worrying about how to manage the separation from her baby when she returned to work after her maternity leave. Questions constantly popped into her head. She was attending to her baby's needs, of course, but felt that a part of her was often distracted or detached from what she was doing in the moment. "I am there with her, absolutely," she told me. "But I also feel like I'm doing this negative daydreaming." It wasn't a new pattern. Her husband, even before the baby arrived, would often say that she was "spinning her wheels" and bemoan her inability to make decisions or definitive plans. "He tells me to let it go or move on all the time. Less thinking, more doing."

Families talk to me about this frequently. Children describe parents who are in the room but not attentive or focusing on what's happening. "It's like she's spacing out a lot," one teen said about her mom. "She's pretending to listen to me, but she's not really listening. I know when she's doing it. I probably do it to her too." Spouses have this complaint as well. "He has this stressed look on his face a lot and says he didn't hear me when I ask him something," one woman told me. When we're ruminating or worrying, absorbed in that inner dialogue, others notice a distant or blank expression.

I know we've all become more accustomed to distracted listening. You're talking to someone, but clearly they're more interested in their phone or otherwise distracted when they respond in a perfunctory way. Or you're nodding as your child is recounting a story while you try to finish that one last email. Handling all the input coming at us is overwhelming. Add our own internal noise, and it's amazing we can tie our shoes some days. But I want you to recognize that you cannot ruminate or worry and be adequately present at the same time. Addressing your RNT patterns *will* improve your relationships.

Ruminating and worrying are common. The vagaries of ordinary modern life offer us plenty of material to masticate. But these patterns, as common as they are, still take a toll, and for most people, these patterns alone aren't necessarily a sign of a diagnosable disorder. But left to fester, these risk factors for anxiety and depression can take you in that direction. Joyce and Brittany were both highly functioning, capable, and successful in many areas of their lives. When they leaned into their RNT, however, it took over. Brittany learned about the patterns and made some changes. (Joyce was not a patient, so I don't know about her.) Recognition, adjustments, and consistent practice worked for Brittany, as they can for you. Small shifts can tip the scales in your favor.

WHAT TO DO

Take In the Big Picture: Process over Content

The first step toward shifting out of RNT is to recognize your patterns, observe how they operate, and acknowledge them as unhelpful habits. This process takes a little leap of faith because it really does *feel* like you're *supposed* to do it—that it is of value. Remember, RNT sets the trap by convincing us we're eating something nutritional when we're actually chewing gum. If I were working with you in therapy, I'd want you to be a better observer of your patterns so that we might create a bit of space between you and RNT. With the help of a little distance, you can become a curious student of RNT, stepping back from the particular details of each episode and noticing the bigger picture. And getting out of the details is crucial. This is how we simplify.

The specifics or details of the worrying and ruminating are the *content*, while the consistent patterns and cycles of worrying and ruminating are the *process*. The content (the stuff, the event, the details of the conversation) is not important because your RNT will grab onto whatever it can find. Most people get mired in the content. But the bigger process of *how* you and your RNT spend time together, *how* your RNT demands your attention, and *how* it keeps you stuck in the spinning wheel of seeking certainty is what you are to observe. What does your RNT repeatedly say? How does it suck you in? What's the generic story it tells? How do you respond? Think of it like a marriage. If a couple constantly gets into brutal arguments over daily stuff (loading the dishwasher, where to eat dinner, the neighbor's dog) but the arguments are filled with name calling, sarcasm, and threats of divorce, the details of the arguments (the content) become far less important than the way the couple communicates or handles disagreements (the process).

For example, a young client of mine is working to recognize and change his RNT process because it prevents him from moving forward. At twenty-seven, he's ready to look for another job, is interested in trying some online dating apps, and wants to begin a long-term investment plan—all very appropriate and common issues to address at this point in his life. But what keeps him immobilized is his habit of going over and over the content of each situation in a search for predecision certainty. He is lousy at making decisions and constantly weighs every option or opinion. Is his boss really that bad? Should he risk leaving this job only to find himself even less satisfied? What did he say on that last date that he shouldn't have said? How will he find a trusted adviser to invest his money? I am helping him recognize how the *process* repeats itself, even though the *particulars* of each situation might differ. Whether it's a boss, a date, or a financial adviser, the pattern is the same.

When we started, he saw his repetitive thinking as the skill that protected him. He sought clarity in order to move forward. He can now better see his RNT as the process that keeps him stuck and a bit miserable. We're getting there.

As you become an expert in your own patterns, notice how predictable, redundant, and persistent these thoughts can be. They are called repetitive and negative for good reason, but they suck you in by behaving like breaking news. You might *feel* activated internally as you think, perseverate, and spin; but remember that worriers and ruminators often engage with their thoughts and *take no action.* When engaged with your RNT, you are less likely to actively implement a solution even when one is presented to you.

Externalize Your RNT Part

Externalizing, or creating a persona for various parts of you, is a way to create that distance and space I addressed earlier. It's a skill I teach to virtually all my anxious and depressed clients, from five to eighty-five. Parts therapy is not new and is used in a variety of ways to help people interrupt destructive patterns, recover from trauma, stay sober, and understand how they move through their lives. Externalizing allows you to both observe this part of yourself with some helpful objectivity and learn to respond to it in new ways. Pull out that ruminating or worrying part of you. Give it a name, a personality, and whatever other characteristics you wish. Make it come alive. Acknowledge it, talk to it, roll your eyes at it. Accept its existence. It's not going to disappear. We all have such a part.

When I met Brittany, the content of her RNT was her baby. Even if she did tend to overthink things in the past, this content was different! She needed to worry about her baby, and no amount of worrying felt like too much. We created a persona for her overthinking part, a version of her grandmother, who she could easily identify as a serious worrier. Brittany recognized that her pattern of overthinking had been there since childhood, and she could "hear" and feel when Mini Gram took over. Of course, becoming a parent was a great opportunity for her RNT to assert its value, but she was able to start shifting her relationship to it. The content (the baby) was new; the process was the same.

Externalizing her worry also helped her marriage. Brittany's husband, Jake, was increasingly frustrated with her negative thinking. When he confronted her about it, she defended the need to keep their baby safe and accused him of not caring enough. These conversations, as you can imagine, never resolved the issue. They were arguing about who loved the baby more, with no understanding of the bigger pattern at play.

But once Brittany owned her RNT and explained it to her husband, they could work as a connected team to usurp the power of Mini Gram. It wasn't always easy. Brittany could feel defensive and embarrassed when Jake called out Mini Gram. Her first instinct was to slip into the particulars again and make the case for her overthinking. Jake could at times be impatient, expecting the pattern to disappear for good rather than accepting the need for ongoing reminders and adjustments. Nonetheless, having a way to talk about the pattern felt less demoralizing for both. It also greatly decreased the conflicts that tended to erupt after visiting with Brittany's family, where Mini Gram's influence was on full display. Denial was replaced with knowing side glances and humor.

When you create your RNT persona, tell your family about it. Give them permission to call you out (in a loving way) when you and your worrying part are holding an exclusive conference. And rather than responding defensively, take a deep breath, then thank your family for their help as you work to change. This will take some practice, I promise you, but it will make a big difference. And if there's a child in your family traveling down the same road, make sure they join in this journey—immediately, not ten years from now when the patterns are well ingrained and substantially more difficult to break.

Embrace Constant Adjustments

Recognition of the pattern and the subsequent shifts you make also require consistent doses of self-forgiveness because you'll need to reset again and again. You don't simply decide to be done with your

RNT and *Poof, it's gone*, because changing pathways in your brain takes repetition as you lay down new track. Your sticky brain won't give up that easily. I love to use metaphors and analogies to inspire understanding or illustrate a point, so I want you to find an example in your life that normalizes this process of resetting or readjusting.

For example, when you drive, you constantly adjust to stay in the lane or manage your speed. If you do yoga, you're always adjusting your postures. If you cook, you taste and adjust the spices. When I ride my bike, I'm always shifting gears. If you sing in a choir or play in an orchestra, you listen and adjust. The list goes on and on. Find the *metaphor of adjustment* that works for you.

Unhook in the Moment

Once you better recognize and understand the process of your RNT, you must start practicing different responses when the thoughts arrive. But let's be real. Forging new paths takes effort. And these brain pathways are well worn and readily available. Our brains like to take the familiar routes. Lessening the frequency and the intensity is the goal, but we still need a strategy to get unstuck when we are pulled in.

I expect the thoughts to grab you at times, as a beginner and even as a pro. You need a *way to unhook*, to simply shift out of the repetitive thinking loop once you get stuck, and there are several ways to go about it. But before I dive into the different methods, a quick reminder: unhooking from your RNT does not mean eliminating your RNT. If you have the expectation that you'll be free of RNT—that you can totally rid yourself of these common and uncomfortable thoughts and feelings—you will be both annoyed with me and frustrated with yourself. Stuff happens, thoughts pop up, elimination strategies backfire.

Because I'm so opposed to the elimination approach, I differentiate between the terms *unhooking* and *distraction,* knowing that distraction is one of the most common techniques for handling RNT; many people are taught to use it as their primary approach. Some distraction can help, but distraction can easily slide into the elimination category if you believe that distraction's goal is to avoid or suppress a thought or feeling. I've had countless people over the years say a version of, "I don't want to think about that, so I've learned to distract myself. I can't go there." I get it, but this type of avoidance says, "I can't handle my thoughts and feelings. . . . I need out!" and often involves distractions that are addictive, disconnecting, or compulsive. Substances, smartphones, gaming, exercise, work—all of these can serve such a role. They become crutches, and you become hobbled. (I'll talk much more about this in chapter 7.)

I prefer the word *unhook* because it sounds to me less urgent and more accepting. I want you to allow those thoughts to show up, recognize the pattern, and then unhook from the repetitive process. And as you unhook, adding that dose of self-compassion is key. Change the message from, "I have to stop thinking about this now. . . . I need to shut my brain off now!" to a less judgmental acknowledgment that you're heading into unproductive territory. Give yourself permission to move forward, away from the negative process:

> I'm getting stuck right now. Time to unhook.
>
> Let me make a shift [remember your adjustment analogy?] so that I can weaken this habit.
>
> This thinking is not valuable or productive.

In the moment, when you feel stuck and trapped, unhook and then pivot to anything that doesn't primarily focus on your own thoughts or feelings or negative physical sensations. Engage in something interesting or enjoyable, even for a few minutes. Ask someone a question about their life or interests. Get curious about something. Listen to great music or do a short (or long) burst of physical activity. Get externally connected in some way, instead of hanging around inside your head, having a meeting with your worry. "Isn't this distraction?" you ask. Sort of, I suppose. But unhooking moves you more gently out of the tug of war in your head. Distraction is often sold as a way to *stop the thinking*. It's just too avoidant for me. Unhooking helps take the edge off your RNT. Worry or rumination can be persistent, like a dog begging for more treats, so be firm and consistent without the intensity. No need to be surprised. It's what RNT and labradoodles do. With time and consistent practice, the thoughts become less demanding and less frequent, so that even when they pop up, they require very little of you.

Do Something!

Action works. If there *is* a problem to be solved, move out of thinking in isolation and ask for help. I was stuck on something recently and clearly spinning it around in my head. I needed another voice to compete with my own, so I called a good friend. We talked it through, and he gave me some steps to take. Nothing complicated, but I needed a little empathy and a kick in the butt to move the project along. Our conversation made me feel better immediately, and doing what he suggested helped enormously. It's an ongoing project, so when I slide into my worries, I repeat the active steps that we discussed. Worriers, in the quest for certainty, often put off getting started while they think more and remain internally focused. I was making that mistake. Start. Get moving. You can adjust as you go. Remember: RNT is not problem solving.

Use That Imagination and Visualize

Research shows that visualization changes the connections and pathways in our brains. Athletes, chronic pain patients, and people with depression and anxiety can all learn to use visual imagery in powerful ways. And after thirty-one years in this business, I can say with confidence that worriers have great imaginations; imagining and visualizing are already in your toolbox. The goal is to create a little video in your mind's eye that illustrates unhooking, whatever that means to you. I like images that shift your thoughts and your mind from sticky to slick, or slow down the thoughts as your ruminating brain spins down.

For example, imagine your RNT as a bike wheel spinning around so fast that the spokes aren't even discernible; then watch as it loses speed and the spokes begin to reappear as the wheel turns more and more slowly.

Or go inside your brain to see the sticky surface of your worried mind. Transform it into a shiny, smooth surface. Shift it from molasses or glue or mud to a cool slab of marble or a shiny jewel. Imagine the stickiest part of your brain becoming slick, allowing the thoughts to slide away. Or go ahead and shrink that gummy part, making it smaller and blurry while you see the problem-solving part growing bigger and more defined.

A client of mine pictured her brain as a busy diner. When she found herself stuck in her RNT, she imagined herself sitting in a booth in her diner-brain, going over the menu again and again but never placing an order. She'd then shift the scene by moving to a different booth. She'd observe herself placing an order, watching as the order was cooked and delivered to her. She enjoyed hearing the ding of the bell as the short-order cook put her plate on the counter for pickup. It was an active, busy visualization, full of movement and substance.

This tool can work in the moment, but you'll want to create the "scene" ahead of time, when you're not in the middle of a stuck cycle. Best to be ready and waiting when you need it. Spend little moments of time with the visualization so that it becomes a more well-worn pathway. (And don't tell me you don't have time. I'm asking for a few seconds here and there throughout the day—and I know how much time you spend ruminating or worrying.) Pull up your image when you're brushing your teeth or washing the shampoo out of your hair, while you're waiting for your dog to pee or sitting at a red light. Take a slow, deep breath, close your eyes, and watch the little clip. Be flexible and change it up if you like. Have fun with it and be creative— because fun and flexibility are the opposite of what sticky brains demand.

If You Can't Sleep

Ruminating and worry are the enemies of sleep, so some specific information and strategies to tackle bedtime RNT are key. If you consider yourself a card-carrying insomniac, or if your sleep problems come and go, chances are good that RNT plays a role. The most obvious circumstance is when you have some stressor you're chewing on. As you settle into sleep, your mind takes you there. It's quiet and isolated. There are no other external obligations to keep your brain occupied. Up pop the thoughts and the accompanying emotions. And then when you can't fall or stay asleep, you start worrying about how not sleeping will impact you the next day. It's a familiar cycle to most of us.

In addition to all the standard strategies, I use the ABC game to unhook my busy brain when I can't fall asleep. First, I remind myself that my body knows how to fall asleep, and I simply need to give my mind something innocuous to chew on for a bit. I pick a mundane topic that I know something about, such as dog breeds or cities in the United States or desserts. (The other night I did dead actresses. I don't know why.) Then I go through the alphabet, spending a few seconds on each letter.

A. Alaskan Malamute

B. Basset hound

C. Corgi

D. Dachshund

If I get stuck on a letter, I move on to the next letter within a few seconds. I don't know any dog breeds or dead actresses that start with the letter X. I sometimes pick a topic and start with the letter M instead of A, mainly because I rarely get to M before falling asleep and I want to change it up. If I go entirely through the alphabet, I start again. Sometimes I pick a number and start subtracting 7: 112, 105, 98, 91, 84—just a little something to chew on. My mind unhooks so my body can do the thing it already knows how to do.

This game is designed to interrupt the thoughts and patterns that keep us thinking. It's a cognitive approach that will do the trick for many of us. If insomnia is a more significant problem for you, either chronically or short-term, I also highly recommend investigating Cognitive Behavioral Therapy for Insomnia (CBT-I). CBT-I is taught in a structured, short-term way. The emphasis is on changing the thoughts about sleep and patterns that keep the insomnia going. It's basically changing your relationship with all things sleep. Studies consistently support CBT-I as a more effective way to deal with insomnia than sleep medications like Ambien. Not surprisingly, taking sleep medication is the most frequently used approach to insomnia—but it is not the most effective, and the side effects when use becomes more long-term are significant, including dependency, impairment in thinking and motor activities during the daytime, daytime drowsiness, increased sleep difficulty, and rebound insomnia. CBT-I results in long-term improvement. You can go to a provider who teaches CBT-I individually or in classes, and many apps and workbooks are also available, including the CBT-i Coach app that was developed by the US Department of Veterans Affairs and is free.

SOME KEY REMINDERS AND A PEP TALK

Finally, I must offer some words of caution that may seem obvious but need to be said directly. Worriers are prone to worrying about their worry. Ruminators will be tempted to go back and ruminate over the impact of their rumination. Now that you have this information, you might fall into the "What have I done?" trap. Here's your first opportunity to practice and observe the tempting pull of judging and stressing about how often you worry whether you've already screwed up your kids with your worrying or how you're going to apologize to your partner, who has been telling you for years that your ruminating was annoying, counterproductive, and sounded just like your mother, and so forth. You will not change this pattern by doing more of the same. That's like yelling at your kids to stop yelling at their siblings. Or eating all the leftover birthday cake for breakfast because it's best to get rid of it so that you don't eat it later. It is simply more of the same: convincing yourself that all thinking—even negative, swirling, painful thinking—is somehow necessary.

The plan is simple:

It's about consistent adjustments.

Small shifts add up to significant positive changes.

You're a work in progress.

The playbook goes like this:

- Recognize you're stuck in an RNT cycle.
- Observe the process and create some distance from that part of you (like Brittany did with Mini Gram).
- If there's a solution or an action to be taken, make a plan and do it. (Constant thinking, reviewing, researching, talking, repeating, and seeking reassurance *are not taking action*. Don't be tricked.)
- After you take action, *unhook*. If there is no action to be taken, acknowledge that fact and *unhook*!
- Practice your visualizations and use them freely to create those new pathways. Employ them in the moment and as you move through your day. Be creative.

I hope I've made this clear: ruminating and worrying happen to all of us. If you have a sticky brain, it happens frequently. Keep at it. Consistently making the adjustments over time is like learning any new skill: riding a bike, learning a language, growing houseplants. As you create these new pathways in your brain, the shifts in your thinking become more automatic. And to get there, you need to do something that sounds a bit strange: look forward to those thoughts arriving because it offers you an opportunity to practice. Paradoxically, counterintuitively, the more you accept their arrival without judgment or resistance, the freer you'll feel. Want proof? Read on.

TAKING RUMINATION UP A MOUNTAIN: A STORY OF SHIFTING GEARS AFTER A CLOSE CALL

A few days after I began working on this chapter, I had a close call, a very near miss. Suddenly I was confronted with the opportunity to work on this ruminating thing as an observer, to notice its power, to see what was possible. Did you ever hear the story about the neuroanatomist Jill Bolte Taylor, who, while in the middle of a stroke at age thirty-seven, began observing what was happening in her brain with the curiosity of a brain expert? It was like that, although my actual experience was far less harrowing than Jill's. (Her journey is chronicled in her 2008 book, *My Stroke of Insight: A Brain Scientist's Personal Journey.*)

My husband and I were headed to a hike in the White Mountains. We were driving on a typical New England two-lane state route, curvy and scenic. Cars travel at speeds from fifty to sixty-five miles per hour. On the side of this road, just short of our chosen trailhead, is a small spring. People often pull over to fill their containers with the cold, pure mountain water. A small parking area for cars makes it an easy and popular stop.

My husband pulled off onto the gravel spot, almost parallel to the road with our car pointing forward, poised to zip back onto the road and head toward the trailhead a few miles ahead. He hopped out of the driver's seat, popped the trunk, and grabbed his big bottle. Off he went while I spaced out in the passenger seat and scrolled on Twitter. Then, both suddenly and slowly, the car began rolling into the road. It's a standard transmission, so evidently it had slipped out of gear. The emergency brake wasn't engaged.

I don't remember exactly what I did those first few seconds. I do know that I looked over my left shoulder and saw a car fast approaching. I think I tried to grab the wheel. I remember bracing for impact. The oncoming driver laid on the horn and swerved around me. I saw another car coming up fast. My car was now almost fully blocking the lane.

Somehow, I jumped into the driver's seat, stretched my legs to depress the clutch, started the car, and screeched out of the way. My husband appeared, confused. Why was I in the road? Was I okay? What was going on?

I told him, tearful now, how the car had just started rolling into the road. "I almost died," I said. Then I said it again.

"You didn't. You're okay," he said. Then we were silent. I was aware of my heart pounding. My hands were in fists. I replayed the scene in my head several times. I added different endings. I began to play what-if.

I can't say what would have happened if we had continued to drive for a longer period of time, just me and my thoughts and the versions of the movie that I was creating. But I knew I'd soon be hiking up a big mountain, one of my favorite activities. I'd be able to discharge the dump of adrenaline that was in my system. Physically, I'd be good. And because of what I do for a living, I also knew that my brain would want to replay those twenty seconds, that I'd be sucked back into the scene again and again.

What could I do? It felt familiar to become the observer, to be curious about these patterns of persistent thought and the pull of imagination. I could practice what I preach as both the clinician and the client, and I wanted to. I reminded myself that this was an opportunity, and I meant to take it. I often tell the families I counsel that viewing our work as an experiment gives us a bit of distance from our own cognitive, emotional, and physical reactions. When we got to the parking lot at the trailhead, I took some breaths, stretched my arms above my head, drank some water, and got to work.

Here's what I did as I hiked:

- I told myself directly, *It's normal for me to go over this. I'm processing this.*
- I reminded myself, *It was terrifying* and *I'm fine, so alternative endings are not necessary.*
- When I noticed myself creating an alternative *what-if* ending, I made a little shift. I came up with the mantra "Of course my brain will drift there. . . . It's okay but no need. No need." I knew I'd do this repeatedly, and that was fine too. While I was hiking, I even said out loud, "Little shift!" and put my attention back to the external world around me.
- Later that day, I consciously thought about *who* would hear this story and who would not. Not my parents, my kids, or my siblings. As I told you at the start, I'm a storyteller (which is a nice way of saying I talk a lot), so thinking about the story and who to tell and then retelling it multiple times could become one of my versions of ruminating. I ultimately decided I would tell my small group of gym friends the next day. I did. That was it. And now you, obviously. (Hi, Mom!)
- I gave myself permission to let the thoughts show up because they were going to anyway. But I didn't need to solve any mystery, fix anything, or ruminate about the alternative endings. That part was done.

- Going forward I'd put on the handbrake in my car when I was parked, except in my driveway. That was action I could take. A solution. Good. Done.
- I told myself that I'd been here before in my life. We all have a "close-call file," and time helps if you gently acknowledge and shift, rather than ruminate or resist.

I worked it—and it worked. It did. The story is there, but it's far less powerful when I stay out of the what-ifs. The initial conscious and fairly frequent reminders are now less intense and less frequent, easier to manage as I write this, three weeks later.

QUESTIONS FOR PONDERING AND JOURNALING
Do you (or others) describe you as an "overthinker"? How has thinking or analysis been seen as valuable? Where did that message originate?
How often does your ruminating seem tied to a feeling of regret? "If only I . . ."
Is journaling a written crutch for perseverating? Or do you process and move on?
Imagine your RNT part. What does it look like, and what are its most frequent statements?
What's your metaphor or visualization for shifting out of your sticky brain?

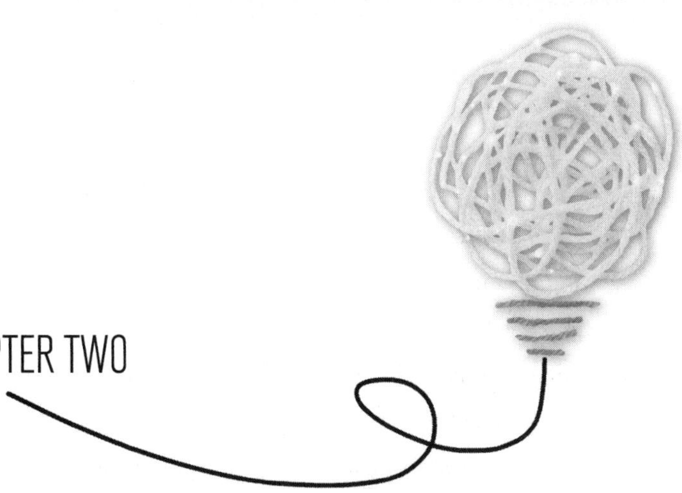

CHAPTER TWO

CATASTROPHES AWAIT

Sneaky Pattern: How Catastrophic Thinking Makes the World a Dangerous Place and Demands You React Accordingly

Could be worse. Not sure how, but it could be.

—Eyore, *Winnie the Pooh*

We cannot solve our problems with the same thinking we used when we created them.

—Albert Einstein

We've already established that worriers have great imaginations. Our next pattern, catastrophizing, also takes advantage of that powerful, creative skill. It's in the family of repetitive negative thinking

(RNT)—because it is clearly repetitive and negative—but some important distinctions make catastrophic thinking more overwhelming, more negative, and at times more difficult to navigate. Let me start by explaining the differences.

Worriers genuinely believe they are looking for solutions. They are future-focused on problems and anticipate bad outcomes, but they see their worry as a path to preventing them. At least that's where they start. The path is often winding and circular, bringing the worrier back to that starting point again and again, like the child in a fairy tale lost in the woods or the characters in a situation comedy who keep arriving at the same place.

Worriers stay on the same path even when it's not taking them anywhere. Their "busy" and sometimes overactive thinking interferes with implementing a solution. Or, when many solutions are offered, worriers resist settling on one course of action. In the absence of the guarantees and reassurance they seek, worriers frequently adopt avoidance as their go-to when the quest for certainty falls short.

Catastrophic thinkers also focus on bad outcomes and often see avoidance as the solution of choice, but compared to worriers, they are a little further down the road. And it's a dark road. This is the neighborhood of worst-case scenarios. Catastrophizers exchange the worrier's "What-if?" for the fatalistic "We're doomed." Catastrophizers experience and talk about the bad outcome as a done deal, a fait accompli. The exaggerated response does not appear to others to be in keeping with the problem, but the catastrophizer is not rationally addressing what's actually happening or even looking at other possible outcomes. It's a distressing misinterpretation of situations or symptoms—an overestimation of the threat.

Most of the patterns throughout this book overlap, and that's absolutely the case here. The worrier sees a potential emergency and wants to avoid it, just like the catastrophizer. But as the worrier plans a trip, she thinks, *I'm really worried we might be late and miss the plane.* She stresses and plans and then acts according to the dictates of her worry. The family arrives at the airport hours earlier than necessary, and she sees her worry as helpful. The catastrophic thinker is also a worrier; however, as she plans the trip, she imagines the family missing their flight, unable to book another one, and forgoing the entire vacation. She goes down the darkest road: her family will never agree to go on vacation again, the money will be wasted, and she'll feel forever responsible for the debacle. In her mind, she strongly believes the worst *will happen* (*or is happening*) and thus reacts with a level of distress equal to this inevitable and terrible outcome.

Catastrophizers are known for making mountains out of molehills. Small incidents are treated as huge problems. The emotional reaction to the perceived threat or worry is overblown, dramatic, and at times unshakable. Life is an emergency. If you relate to this, you know it's an exhausting way to live. You create and subject yourself to your own waking nightmares. And if you were raised in such an environment, it also left a mark. This is a family pattern—strong in some family cultures and traditions—that needs to be interrupted. I discuss that later in the chapter.

If becoming absorbed in these nightmares is so painful, why do people do it? First, this kind of thinking—imagining the worst-case scenario—can feel protective. If I go to the worst-case scenario—if I let myself imagine how it will play out—then I'll be prepared. I've also heard many people argue in support of imagining the worst so that when it *doesn't* happen, they'll be delightfully surprised. Prepare for the worst and hope for the best, they say. And there is, I suppose, a case to be made for this type of "preventative" thinking, if it leads you to act in proportion to the threat. Let's call that "preemptive catastrophic thinking possibly with problem solving." Is it possible? Sometimes.

For example, during the pandemic, we all heard about worst-case scenarios, ranging from the inconvenient (running out of toilet paper) to the terrible (running out of food or medical equipment) to the horrific (family members dying alone in the ICU). Many of us took action to prevent such outcomes: stocking up on supplies, buying an extra freezer to store food, staying away from family members who were at greatest risk. All these actions were reasonable responses to a threat. We felt anxious and at times overwhelmed; we heard the threatening information, assessed it, and went into action. However, if you heard the threats, repeatedly imagined your family suffering terrible consequences, and even after taking some action remained haunted by the inevitability of the outcome, you were catastrophizing. If your decisions, conversations, and emotions were all filtered through your sad, scary, nightmarish outcome, you were catastrophizing.

Second, we all do this catastrophic imagining to some degree because we are social beings. When we hear about someone's story and put ourselves into their shoes, this creates empathy and connection. When I learn about someone close to my age receiving a cancer diagnosis or when a friend gets in a biking accident (because I bike), I take their story and put myself into it. I feel sympathy for them and also imagine what it would be like if it were me. That's normal. If I told you my cat died and you loved your pet, you would, I hope, empathically feel some of my pain as you imagined your own pet dying or remembered your own experience. You might even decide to keep your cat in at night after hearing what happened to mine or make the full jump to indoor cat.

But if you become absorbed in the story, imagine your own pet's demise over and over, need to know where your pet is every minute, and cry regularly about its impending death, you're catastrophizing. If you come home from work and your cat doesn't greet you at the door and you then immediately freak out, you're catastrophizing.

THE DISGUISE OF COMMON CATASTROPHIC TERRITORY

I said this in the last chapter and I say it again now: the specific content of any anxious pattern is not all that important to me. When you're working to break out of your anxious patterns, it's process, not content, that will move you forward. It's the big picture, not the details. I also know that staying out of the details of catastrophic imaginings can be particularly difficult because the path to worst-case scenarios is often paved with content that is both common and emotionally loaded.

From parenting to pain, some catastrophic paths quickly connect us to inevitable human experiences, so it's harder to escape them. Certain categories, certain content, show up powerfully and frequently. Consider them the *Catastrophizer's Greatest Hits*. I give examples here not because these subjects need to be treated differently (quite the opposite!) but because they're so common. Their prevalence can make them sneaky; you might not even know you're going there. Catastrophizing about certain things might feel natural and automatic, even socially endorsed. If you relate to any of them, you're in good company, but that is all the more reason to pay attention to their pull. This is how we demystify.

Health and Physical Symptoms

Catastrophic thinking about physical health is commonly referred to as *hypochondria*, although the more modern and accurate diagnostic terms are "somatic symptom disorder" or "illness anxiety disorder." With or without this diagnostic language, these terms simply describe a preoccupation with symptoms you notice or worries about illnesses that you could possibly get, even if you aren't experiencing any symptoms. Small symptoms are imagined to be signs of serious, catastrophic illness. You notice a twitching in your eye and within minutes you've planned for your inevitable blindness or funeral. Famous hypochondriacs include Charles Darwin, Howard Hughes, and Florence Nightingale. Ferris Bueller's friend Cameron, trapped in his house, believing he was near death due to allergies, is one of many fictional characters with this issue. People who catastrophize about their physical health seek medical attention often, looking for both reassurance that nothing is wrong and validation that something is wrong. It's exhausting and can have significant impact on mood, anxiety levels, and relationships.

For example, Rebecca, a capable and outgoing woman in her late thirties, was referred by her doctor because of her catastrophic thinking about illness. If she experienced any kind of symptom, she became immediately convinced that something was terribly wrong and reacted with panic. A headache was a brain tumor; a cough was lung cancer; when she forgot the first name of an acquaintance in the grocery store, it was surely early-onset Alzheimer's.

In the early years of her relationship with her husband, he would gently point out that her reactions seemed overblown. She became angry at his suggestions, so he soon supported her frequent visits to the doctor, hoping over time that a consistent clean bill of health would change the pattern. The doctor also believed that repeated "false alarms" would interrupt the pattern, so he would kindly perform test after test, letting her know that he would always take her concerns seriously and provide the reassurance she needed. However, his willingness to respond to every catastrophic thought combined with his hesitancy to address the pattern directly only made Rebecca worse. When she began to play out the same catastrophic patterns with her children, the doctor urged her to see me.

When Rebecca and I looked together at the bigger picture of her anxiety, we could see that her concerns about illness—although the most prominent of Rebecca's catastrophic thoughts and actions—weren't the only content to which her worst-case thinking gravitated. She was able to see the pattern as a well-worn, practically reflexive pathway in her imagination. We also tackled the issue of modeling catastrophic thinking with her children; not surprisingly it was a generational pattern that she experienced in her family growing up. Overreaction was modeled for her; the options of patience, observation, and problem solving—and when to apply them—were not.

Pain

Interestingly, one of the most researched areas of catastrophic thinking involves pain because of the high cost of chronic pain in a wide range of domains. The Pain Catastrophizing Scale (PCS) has been used for decades to look at how people catastrophically respond to pain and how it impacts their recovery, activity levels, and the likelihood they'll end up on disability. Those who score high on the PCS ruminate about their pain, worry that something is seriously wrong with them, fear that something serious might happen if they engage in life activities, and feel helpless to do anything to deal with their pain. They talk about and perceive their pain through a worst-case lens. Sadly, most become trapped in a cycle of vigilance, overreactivity, and fear, all of which ultimately increase their pain levels, ironically the very thing they are trying to avoid.

Studies find that people going into surgery with catastrophic predictions of their postsurgical pain are more likely to develop chronic pain conditions. Such thinking and the subsequent reactions to those catastrophic thoughts have been shown to negatively impact lower-back pain, childbirth, and quality of life for migraine sufferers. One study found that a single question assessing catastrophic pain response was a predictor of opioid misuse in chronic pain patients.

Researchers are also acutely interested in the family processes related to childhood pain, including the role of a parent's catastrophic thinking. An abundance of evidence points to a connection between parental catastrophizing about a child's pain and a higher degree of disability, lower participation in activities, and decreased attendance at school. Importantly, these outcomes are separate from the child's own reported pain intensity. The parent's catastrophizing, not the child's perception and reporting of their own pain, has the greater impact. In other research, Goubert and Simons found that catastrophic parents were more distressed, more protective, and paid more attention to the pain, which ultimately resulted in more pain and disability in the child.

When you're catastrophizing about pain, this does not mean the pain isn't real. But your catastrophic fears about the pain—whether or not you will ever get better, the severity of what's wrong with you, or your belief the pain will get worse and worse—are key factors that determine what you do about your pain and how you live your life. If you believe your pain will worsen no matter what you do, you will make certain decisions about treatment, activities, and your future. If you believe that your pain is treatable or manageable, that you have some agency in how you respond to your pain and its course, your recovery will be quite different.

I experienced this firsthand several years ago when I hurt my back while reaching to pick up a heavy box. I've had many injuries, but not being able to bend over to tie my shoes without significant pain freaked me out. I started imagining the worst. What was wrong with me? What if I could never hike or bike or run again? I could feel the panic grabbing hold.

I was teaching indoor cycling at the time, and lucky for me, my friend and physical therapist, Sue, took my class. When I walked into class gingerly and announced I'd be teaching off the bike, she asked me several questions. Then she got me into her office the next day. She gave me several stretches and exercises. I stood up in my office while seeing clients and, between appointments, did the stretches and exercises she gave me.

The exercises helped tremendously. But what helped me most was this: Sue confidently told me she knew what the problem was and how to fix it. She also knew how to help me prevent it from happening again. And she said, "If you ever feel this pain again, you now know what it is and how to handle it. No need to panic." It was as if she were talking directly to my catastrophic part, taking away its power and allowing me to take the action I needed to heal. I believed her. My back has been great for years, but most importantly I have handled any expected tweaks with knowledge and confidence. I am forever grateful.

Catastrophizing Fear Itself

Some people get catastrophic about being anxious. This pattern of thinking increases the severity of certain types of anxiety and even helps push anxiety into depression. This isn't surprising, of course. You can be catastrophic about most anything, so being catastrophic about feeling anxious seems rather predictable. There's even a term for this: *anxiety sensitivity.* Anxiety sensitivity refers to an overreaction to the physical symptoms of anxiety, believing these sensations to be dangerous or harmful. This misinterpretation of symptoms only causes the anxiety and its patterns to intensify, just as we saw with pain.

For example, if you have anxiety sensitivity and you notice your heart is pounding as you prepare for a presentation or an uncomfortable confrontation with your neighbor, you will *not* interpret your pounding heart as a reasonable and normal reaction, but as an impending heart attack. Instead of saying to yourself, *Well, I'm so nervous that my heart is pounding,* you say, *I think I'm having a heart attack. . . . Obviously I can't have this conversation now!* and then you avoid the conversation and freak out over your potential catastrophic demise—which only makes your heart rate faster and your avoidance fiercer. You start focusing on what's wrong with you. And the more you feel frightened, hopeless, and exhausted by your unremitting symptoms, the more likely you are to become depressed. The more anxious you feel, the more you avoid and disconnect. Your world gets smaller. Your worst-case scenario is coming true. Your negative expectations are met—and then some.

In his 1933 inaugural address, Franklin Roosevelt spoke of this exact phenomenon, addressing the collective catastrophizing of a nation that he wanted to activate and move forward. Most of us are familiar with the first part of his "fear itself" statement, but the full sentence is illuminating: "So, first of all, let me assert my firm belief that the only thing we have to fear is fear itself—nameless, unreasoning, unjustified terror which paralyzes needed efforts to convert retreat into advance."

Sound familiar? The more your catastrophic patterns have a say in how you live your life, the more powerless and hopeless you feel. The more hopeless you feel, the less productive action you take. The spiral intensifies.

Sleep

As I described in the previous chapter, thinking too much and falling asleep aren't compatible. And thinking about not falling asleep as you're trying to fall asleep is a particularly quick descent into anxious spinning. Whether you are ruminating, worrying, or catastrophizing as you try to sleep, the result is often the same: not sleeping well. Refer back to page 27 in chapter 1 for specific strategies to unhook from your stuck thinking during those times when you can't fall asleep.

Additionally, pay attention to the catastrophic predictions or statements you may be consistently making about you and sleep. Do you refer to yourself as a horrible sleeper? Do you predict and fear that you won't be able to fall asleep? Has this become a part of your identity? I once worked with Joe, a self-described insomniac who spoke so catastrophically about sleep that I wondered how his poor brain and body stood any chance of falling asleep each night. "It's horrible," he told me. "Every night as I start to get ready for bed, or even hours ahead of time, I just know that I'm going to be in for hours of torture." He clearly accepted this as a permanent affliction and almost automatically catastrophized about how his lack of sleep would impact him both short-term and long-term, telling me, "If I have a big project the next day, I know I won't be able to focus and everyone will see I'm exhausted," and "I've read the research on how bad a lack of sleep is for your health. . . . I'm doomed."

Interestingly, Joe's wife often told him that he truly did sleep when he complained in the morning of "not sleeping a wink." This isn't surprising because research shows that many insomniacs are rather lousy at gauging how much they sleep. Most subjects consistently underestimate the amount of time they sleep and overestimate the amount of time it takes them to fall asleep, in comparison with what laboratory data reveal during a sleep study. People with this pattern of sleep misperception tend to be more anxious and ruminative in general. They have more intrusive thoughts and worry catastrophically about sleep. As with pain, the worry is not a way out of sleep problems; it pulls you in deeper.

Joe, like Rebecca and her health-related catastrophizing, was able to look at his broader pattern and see it as more pervasive than just around his sleep. He learned, in fact, that he misperceived a lot of things in his life, jumping to negative conclusions that kept him locked in an overreactive and painful emotional cycle. Whenever his supervisor asked to meet with him, he immediately assumed he was going to be fired. Whenever his phone rang or a text came in, he felt a reflexive pang of dread. To change this pattern, Joe first worked to stop identifying and talking about himself as an insomniac. He began to catch his catastrophic predictions about his sleep, which he realized were particularly pervasive. I was so glad to have his wife's input and historical perspective, and ultimately so was Joe. It helped him see the catastrophic patterns in his own parents and recognize the impact on his wife and kids. He also really needed to hear that she noticed the changes he was making and how these changes benefitted the whole family. Making new pathways requires patience and support.

You know where I'm going with this, don't you?

THE FAMILY THAT CATASTROPHIZES TOGETHER . . .

The power of family modeling, not surprisingly, shows up here. How we view and respond to life's circumstances comes in large part from the modeling of our caretakers and the familial and broader culture that surrounds us. For some families, being negatively catastrophic is part of their daily routine, part of the worldview—so much so that you don't even notice or question it! Catastrophic families don't sit around and talk about how to be less catastrophic. If families do acknowledge it, it's often in the vein of, "That's who we are," or, "We come by it honestly." There might be some humor or teasing, but the very nature of being catastrophic doesn't lend itself to much optimism about changing the pattern: "We might be catastrophic, but in this world, who wouldn't be?"

The expression of fear by loving adults in front of or directly to children is a powerful risk factor for childhood anxiety, similar to how it impacts childhood pain. It's no surprise that children raised in anxious families perceive the world as a more dangerous place than children raised in nonanxious families. And because they are often an audience to the predictive bad-outcome videos of daily life, they have difficulty assessing risk in a reasonable way. This plays right into anxiety's playbook: seek certainty and comfort, but in its absence, *avoid.*

If you are a catastrophic parent, chances are you focus on the dangers of life in well-meaning attempts to protect your family. But remember, catastrophic thinking carries that dark cloud of inevitability. It's going to happen! We're doomed! For some families, there's a superstitious element to this type of dire predicting. I remember talking to a pregnant friend about the ease of her pregnancy. How great for her, I smiled. "But," she said, "we all know that when things are going too well, that's a sign something bad is going to happen." I grimaced internally (I think, I hope), imagining how this would translate into parenting once that baby arrived. You'll recall this was the case in Rebecca's young family; it was the impact of her patterns on her children that concerned her doctor enough to shift his approach, referring her for help.

This doesn't mean you should abandon all safety precautions. This is not an all-or-nothing proposition. You don't let your kids do whatever they want and hope it goes well. (I'll talk specifically about all-or-nothing, global thinking in the next chapter.) As parents, we offer the instructions that help our children learn, especially when they're little or stepping into new developmental territory like starting school, staying home alone for the first time, or learning to drive. We remain present and supportive.

As you allow your child to partake in an activity or take a step toward more independence, you should do two things at once: accept that catastrophic thoughts might pop up *and* let go of the compunction to narrate the possible horrible outcomes that your family is narrowly averting. No one can enjoy the activity accompanied by this play-by-play: "Okay, everyone . . . I see poison ivy around here and it's terrible if we get it. And let's also watch for hornets and tics. They might bite you, so you need to stay close to me so we can stay safe and have fun." Instead, try saying, "Okay, let's keep an eye out for poison ivy. See what it looks like?" Then do a tick check when you get home, like we New Englanders do routinely these days.

As I was writing this chapter, I checked in with my mother, whose maiden name is Cathleen Marie Murphy. She's rather an expert on catastrophic thinking, having been raised in a large Irish Catholic family who, she told me, treated everything as an emergency. She's also a Murphy, and Murphy's Law states, "Anything that can go wrong will go wrong," the same sentiment expressed by my pregnant friend. Having heard this phrase all my life, I assumed it was an old Irish proverb. I was surprised to discover that it's attributed to Edward Murphy, an aerospace engineer, who coined the phrase in the early 1950s. Perhaps he had the same type of catastrophic upbringing, so when his equipment failed, this explanation was the most familiar.

My mother was the youngest of four, and her mother, Helen, one of eight. "They always predicted the worst was going to happen," she said of her mother and seven siblings. And when it did, there was plenty of blaming. "I told you so" was a favorite refrain. Once when my mother was about eight or nine years old, her cousin Joanne got a new bike. As my mother ran down the road, excited to give it a try, my grandmother yelled after her, "Don't you ride that bike! You'll fall and get hurt!" My mother did ride the bike and she did fall and cut her knee. "I told you so" was my grandmother's response.

I also asked about another family motto, "Too much laughing turns to crying." I heard it referenced often but never knew its origins. "My aunt Irene [the youngest] was being tickled and laughing and laughing," my mother told me. "And then later that day she had a stomachache and it turned out to be appendicitis. See? We were all laughing and look what happened!" Tragedy, she said, was always around the corner, and this was simply more proof.

When children are soaked in a constant stream of safety and doomsday chatter, reminded of the horrible outcomes that will inevitably occur, the result is often an anxious child who cannot or will not step out into the world. And it's a tough way to parent too. When you anticipate the worst, when does your mind get to rest? How do you enjoy time with your children? And how do you teach your children to make their own assessments and move forward in life when you dominate them with your own catastrophic point of view? How do you want to view the passage through life? As a series of catastrophes to avoid—or something different?

Historic family patterns are hard to break, especially when you don't have the necessary distance to gain perspective. It's time to adopt another view.

WHAT TO DO

Review the RNT Strategies and Suggestions in Chapter 1

I don't know if I've ever met a "pure" catastrophizer who doesn't also engage in some ruminating and worrying. Review pages 29–30 and see what also applies to your catastrophizing. Much of it will.

Some reminders:

- Consider externalizing your catastrophic part to create that helpful distance and better recognize the bigger patterns, as well as inject a bit of playfulness and humor into the mix.
- Remember that addressing the content of each specific catastrophic situation is how you remain catastrophic. Being aware of how you welcome the catastrophic view of life is essential to shifting it. Focusing on the details of your imaginings entices you into missing the bigger pattern.
- Small and consistent adjustments matter as you work to develop these new thought pathways. Expect and allow the thoughts to appear—then consciously unhook. Keep at it. It usually takes time to shift patterns, but also allow for coveted epiphany moments. You might be working to interrupt or push back against a long history of catastrophizing.

Additionally, these catastrophic-specific tips can help.

Pay Close Attention to Catastrophic Language

Catastrophizing, often more than the internal processes of worrying or ruminating, happens out loud. Catastrophizers like to predict the inevitable catastrophe and then reconfirm the validity of their pessimism. As with my mother's family, the postgame gloating serves as vindication of their worldview. Writer Niedria Dionne Kenny asked, "Wouldn't it be nice if people could keep their rain on their own parade?" Catastrophizers don't.

Be aware that sharing your catastrophic predictions—often accompanied by your catastrophic retelling of tragedies—gets in the way of assessing risk in the moment. Using the example of dogs, announcing to your family members, "Dogs bite," will support avoidance of dogs, thus limiting where you go and your enjoyment of many social and recreational activities—and helpful exposure to friendly dogs! Reminding your family of how your childhood friend was bitten in the face by a dog whenever your family encounters a dog creates a vivid movie in everyone's imagination to back up the belief that dogs are dangerous. If that sounds like you, stop it!

I had a friend whose family always ended their conversations on the phone saying, "I love you." Every conversation. It was nice, I thought, and I pointed it out to my friend. "Oh, that's because our mom wants to make sure that if we die or get killed or something, those will be our last words to each other." Yikes. They might as well have been saying, "In case I meet my demise in the next hour, I love you." The expression of love is great, but let's lose the catastrophic side dish. We want to offer solid safety instruction (good!) without the scary explanation that follows (not good!).

Talk Directly and Matter-of-Factly About Changing the Pattern

If you are working on changing your catastrophic patterns, let your loved ones know. Together start to observe the pervasiveness of catastrophic language around you. It's often easier to recognize catastrophic language coming out of someone else's mouth rather than our own (true for most of these anxious patterns and for human behaviors in general), so practice by noticing those words from others as well as yourself.

Does your local news station have a catastrophic weather forecaster? What about alarmist clickbait and headlines? Who are your most catastrophic family members and friends? Giving your children permission to point out your dire proclamations assures you will receive notice because they absolutely hear them.

I asked people to share examples of this in their families, and Kelly described her mother's catastrophic announcements: "Anytime my mom left the house or left my brother and me in the car, she would always say, 'I'm going to lock the door so nobody steals you.' She didn't know it, but I was terrified of being stolen! My brother and I are adults now, and she told me her biggest fear when I was a kid was one of us being kidnapped! Um, I think we knew that, Mom." Kelly still locks all her doors—which may be a fine strategy based on where she lives, the crime rates, and so on—but the goal is that this type of decision results from updated data and problem solving rather than the remnants of a catastrophic family legacy.

Practice Problem-Solving Language Instead

Catastrophic thinkers tend to focus on what they don't want to happen. They are truly living a negative life of what not to do. When they approach or consider situations, they imagine disaster. If you are catastrophic, you likely mistake this type of thinking for problem solving. Like RNT, it's not—which means you may need to work harder at using problem-solving language with yourself and others. To start, know that your automatic flash of negative outcomes will pop up, but your job is to recognize that habit of yours, keep those thoughts to yourself, and then follow up with a constructive action.

I recall a particularly instructive coach when my boys played Little League. His experience started with telling the kids what *not to do*: don't use one hand to catch (you'll drop the ball), stop swinging at every pitch (you'll strike out), don't stroll to first (they will throw you out). It took some time, a season or two, to shift his chatter (and that of the kids on the team) toward *what to do*: match your swing to the pitch, use both hands to contain the ball in your mitt, be alert to steal second, if the ball passes the catcher, hit the mitt! The kids played better and had more fun.

Let's take the example of approaching a dog from the perspective of a problem solver instead of a catastrophizer. Talk about and then model how approaching an unknown dog requires certain steps, including observing the dog's behavior, asking the owner about the dog, then making a reasonable judgment: "That dog looks friendly, doesn't it? Let's ask and see if we're right." Or, "That dog is barking and jumping. I wonder if we should keep our distance." Or, "That dog is growling and looks angry. I'm keeping my distance and looking for a big stick."

Robin, my sister-in-law and podcast partner, is a professional travel adviser. She recommends that all travelers have a little pouch stocked with basic medicines and first-aid supplies, a stash that enables you to easily respond when getting to a pharmacy or a doctor proves difficult. It's a part of her own routine, and once it's done, she doesn't talk about it or even think much about it. What would the catastrophic person do? She'd constantly open the pouch and check the contents, or research online what possible malady could happen while in a particular place. She might even talk (a lot) about what she's adding and why.

Problem-solving language means discussing what you want to happen, rather than what you are fearful of happening. Instead of saying, "Watch out! That bee will sting you!" you might announce once or twice, "Pay attention to that bee. He's happier if you give him space." Instead of saying, "If you drive like that, you're gonna kill yourself!" say, "I want you to pay attention when you drive. It's your responsibility to follow the rules of the road." You also need to talk less, giving your brain and those around you time to problem solve, to think and assess. I routinely tell my anxious clients they need to talk 85 percent less as they address a problem. Lose the safety chatter.

As our boys were growing up, my husband would say to them, "Think one step ahead." Rather than describing what we didn't want them to do (prompting them to play out that little negative movie in their minds), we wanted to model and encourage problem solving, to create a picture of action rather than fear. As they grew older, we allowed them to problem solve more independently. Instead of reminding them that the world was a dangerous place, we wanted to develop their ability to assess cause and effect, to manage reasonable risk. They are young adults now, and it hasn't always gone well. Problem solving almost always includes a problem, and teenage brains resist this type of cause-and-effect thinking. But the seeds were planted and nurtured, and the foundational skills are there.

Lose the catastrophic words and lengthy stories you reflexively say as they head out the door, those conveying that some disaster awaits, such as the following:

- Be careful!
- Don't talk to strangers!
- Text me as soon as you get there!
- Remember what happened to Uncle Paul!

Instead, come up with a problem-solving mantra for your family that predicts, or at least makes room for, a good outcome:

- Think one step ahead.
- Have fun and pay attention.
- Use your brain. It's a good one.
- I can't wait to hear about your adventure!
- Work on those smart choices.

Don't Mistake Catastrophizing for Being Realistic

People who are catastrophic and pessimistic about outcomes tend to dismiss others' optimism as foolish or negligent. They can even be rather condescending, as if looking at situations positively makes someone a sucker or unintelligent. I hate to say it, but being overly pessimistic (or overly optimistic also) indicates a tendency to ignore valuable information. Not so smart. A friend was describing his frustration with a catastrophic relative who, he said, "is programmed to obsess." All the presented evidence falls on deaf ears, and the catastrophic projections are treated "as if they are actually happening right now." In the eyes of this catastrophic relative, my friend is seen as naïve, and his attempts to help are dismissed. How silly to believe that things might go well!

Working on your catastrophic patterns doesn't require an embrace of toxic positivity or a denial of life's risks. We don't need to swing fully in the opposite direction. Some dogs do bite, and kids do fall off bikes. You just don't need to be the self-appointed reminder of all that's bad and tragic, nor the predictor and cataloguer of life's inevitable disappointments.

Stop Tracking

For the past several years, I've strongly recommended that parents stop using tracking apps on their phones, such as Life 360. And I've been urging them to let go of the constant checking and notifications they receive from school-based portals like Power School and Aspen. I have many reasons for this stance, but they all lead back to the need for kids to develop autonomy, better communication skills, and the ability to problem solve. Adults who watch a child's every move are conveying a lack of trust in the child and the world, while not allowing the child opportunities to work the autonomy muscle. I've also seen an increase in children tracking their parents and adults tracking each other. More disturbing is the trend of teen couples tracking each other as a way to prove they aren't cheating or lying. This desire or even demand to know another's exact location is often a warning sign, an indicator in a relationship of jealousy, possessiveness, and potentially abusive control.

If you are catastrophic, tracking amplifies your need for certainty (because bad things happen) and your ability to take ambiguous information and overreact fearfully to it. *Did my daughter walk home safely from school? Why did my partner stop there? Is he lying to me? Whose house is my son at right now? Is my daughter in her dorm room or someone else's? And what if something happens to* me? *I want people to know where I am.*

I've heard all the reasons why tracking is convenient, efficient, and necessary for safety. In fact, there are few things I recommend that get as much pushback as this! But keep in mind that catastrophic people see the world as dangerous and convey that attitude to the people they love. If you are a catastrophic tracker, you'll jump to the most dramatic and dangerous conclusions with the data provided. Of course, you can also do this without tracking. When your partner is ten minutes late, you can conclude she's in a ditch or doing something terrible. But rather than eliminating your internal impulse to focus on worst-case scenarios, using a tracking app will feed it and strengthen it.

As I said earlier, children raised by worried parents perceive the world as a more dangerous place and project danger onto ambiguous situations. I've had many discussions with anxious parents who see this as a good thing. They want their children to be cautious, fearful, and vigilant because—they tell me—it will keep them safe. Scaring them works. However, fear can invite avoidance. The inability to assess reasonable risk only supports the anxious and depressing worldview that is now epidemic in teens and young adults.

Have Some Fun! Play!

After hearing many new details from my mother about her catastrophic clan, I asked her how she was able to move away from the mindset of her upbringing. Her dream, she said, "was to have fun with my own family." She didn't give it much conscious thought as a young mother, but she knew her own family rarely had fun. My father's family also didn't create or value fun. "So I took over fun. And I had to keep doing it. We would have fun among all the human screwups. . . . It helped us get through the tough times. 'Fun' was the guiding word."

This may seem like an obvious statement, but catastrophic thinking is incompatible with fun. Off to the beach? Sharks! Riptides! Blistering sunburn! A picnic? Ticks! Allergies! Thunderstorms! I remember a meeting with a mom and daughter many years ago. As I started to describe catastrophic thinking, they looked at each other and laughed. "We are catastrophic packers!" the mom said. "For every trip we go on, I imagine the worst thing that could happen and pack for it." While the family might be excited to go camping, the discussions and preparation leading up to the vacation were filled with those terrible imagined movie clips, ranging from diarrhea to blisters to dislocated kneecaps. Fun!

During the heights of the Covid pandemic, the word *safe* was much more important than the word *play.* Along with so much else, we lost play. It was too risky. People even began to see any suggestion of play as irresponsible and dangerous. For example, during the pandemic, I was a regular on the local news. Every few weeks, an anchorperson would interview me for advice to help families deal with stress and other big emotions. Almost always, I included a strong suggestion to get outside and move. I encouraged families to be silly and playful. On one summer segment, I told people to go pick blueberries. (It's a thing here in New Hampshire.) Someone who saw the broadcast found my email and fired off a furious screed. I was ridiculous, he wrote. How dare I suggest picking blueberries! This was professional advice? I should have my license revoked! Sir, wherever you are, I stand by my advice for families to play. Fun was hard to come by during the pandemic, and paradoxically more important than ever. And it still is.

When children play, they are developing social skills, executive functioning, independence, self-regulation, fine and gross motor skills, and language. They are also testing boundaries and failing as they develop new behaviors. Taking reasonable risks is an important part of the experience, and some countries are recognizing its value. In a 2018 *New York Times* article about playgrounds in England, writer Ellen Barry described a movement away from risk aversion to more opportunities for children to develop resilience and grit: "Britain is one of a number of countries where educators and regulators say a litigious, protective culture has gone too far, leaching healthy risks out of childhood. Guidelines on play from the government agency that oversees health and safety issues in Britain state that 'the goal is not to eliminate risk.'" Schools in Australia, Canada, and Sweden are adopting similar approaches. The United States, because of litigation fears, has not followed the trend.

Do you allow your family—and yourself—to have fun? How do you play? Not just as a parent or caretaker, but *you*? How do you play as an adult with your friends and your partner? What does that look like? Do you make room for joy and fun and risk? How often does it happen? What is your tolerance for risk? Who is the narrator of potential disaster?

Remember, it's not all or nothing. You can give the people around you information and some warnings. If you find out that alpine ski racers have a 100 percent major injury rate (knees, backs, shoulders, necks), you might want to consider safer competitive sporting activities. You can take reasonable precautions. Also, though, you can limit your predictions of doom. And if something does go awry, work on changing those big emotional reactions, which often include dramatic announcements filled with blame, regret, and future restrictions. "I told you this was a bad idea! We never should have come! And we'll never do something this risky again!" This pattern of big, all-or-nothing reactions is another sneaky pattern that bolsters anxiety and dampens your enjoyment of life. It is referred to as a global attributional style, or global thinking, and it's the subject of the next chapter.

QUESTIONS FOR PONDERING AND JOURNALING
In your own family, who was catastrophic? Who allowed you to take reasonable risks?
Is "safety chatter" a part of your family's experience, that is, constant reminders about the hazards and dangers of activities?
Is there an impact on you or your relationships, from your upbringing or internal monologue, due to catastrophic language and avoiding?
Write down four or five statements that you might say to your family that would support *movement with responsibility* versus *fearful avoidance*. ("I need you to think a step ahead before you go out on that ice. How will you determine if it's a good decision?")
Did your family know how to have fun? What's fun and joyful for you now? Do you participate in any activities that involve some risk, but you do them anyway because of the enjoyment they give you?

CHAPTER THREE

GOING GLOBAL

Sneaky Pattern: How Big Conclusions and an All-or-Nothing Approach Make the World Smaller and Harder to Navigate

Do your little bit of good where you are; it's those little bits of good put together that overwhelm the world.

—Desmond Tutu

When something happens in your life, how do you explain it? Do you factor in the specifics of the situation, or do you stick to one explanation regardless of the circumstances? Do you see yourself as consistently the victim of circumstance or overly responsible for outcomes?

How you come to conclusions about yourself, the world, and other people is referred to as your attributional style. And if you tend to come to big conclusions—and stick with them—or employ broad brushstrokes in place of details or variety, then your style is described as "global." With such a style, a person uses global language, peppering conclusions with words like *never* and *always.*

We'll never get out of this mess.

Nobody will ever love me.

People always disappoint, so I don't trust them.

Nothing that person says is worth listening to.

If you're a global thinker, you may be prone to all-or-nothing thinking (*My house is either immaculate, or it's an embarrassing mess*). You might label others or yourself in general ways based on a single encounter or an assumption, without acknowledging the context of the encounter or variability in people's personalities (*All librarians are introverted*). Or you tend to overgeneralize outcomes based on very few experiences or focus on the negative aspects of an experience (*Vacations just aren't relaxing*, or *Nobody makes good tomato soup anymore*).

Global thinking is big: big conclusions, big problems, big avoidance. Reactions and decisions are based on broad, emotional, or unexamined assumptions that leave you feeling trapped and overwhelmed. And like all the other anxious patterns, this global pattern enjoys company. It revels in the opportunity to join with catastrophic, negative, avoidant thinking, even in a single statement.

Every time I make plans with people, I end up freaking out and cancelling.

Crowds are terrifying, so I'm not going to the concert.

I always test horribly, so why bother to take the course?

We're doomed.

Global thinking has a hopeless, passive tone to it. You overestimate the problem in front of you, then feel helpless to do anything about it. The result is a sense of fear or panic, followed by shutting down, a retreat. We already know that anxiety is a fast track to depression, and this pattern of global thinking is a vivid example of how anxiety and depression so closely overlap. It can influence many areas of your life. The good news? When you interrupt this pattern, the positive impact is powerful.

GLOBAL ISOLATIONISM

Such was the case with Lucia, a middle-schooler I met a few years ago. Lucia had always been very anxious about fitting in and being liked by others, but it really came to a head when she entered seventh grade. By mid-October, she regularly refused to attend school, missing at least two days a week. Her reports of school days were filled with global language: *Nobody likes me, all my teachers hate me, I'll never fit in.* Because she was so worried about what others thought, she and her worry formed quick and negative conclusions that then supported her avoidance of school, which allowed her to perpetuate her global conclusions. So it went. With no intervention, I'm certain she would have become depressed within her first two years of high school. Her anxiety was preventing her from participating academically and socially, and without help she'd continue to fall behind further and further. Her isolation would increase.

Lucia's parents convinced her to meet me. She also had global thoughts about therapists. She was sure, her mother told me, that I would be annoying and wear sandals with socks and use phrases like, "Say more about that." When she showed up in my office—not happily at first—I worked hard to defy her global ideas of therapy and therapists. Step by step, we worked on her anxious patterns. We worked on shifting her habit of jumping to global conclusions, paying a tiny bit of attention to the content of each internal global announcement, but mainly looking at its redundant process. Stepping back and questioning her own thinking were key skills for her to learn.

She's doing well now because the phrases she uses when she's "going global" are easy for her and her parents to recognize: *I'll never figure this out. I'm a loser. Nobody gets me.* The pattern arrives when she is most stressed, often when she feels uncertain in new situations. Because it works to keep her disconnected and passive, she now knows this point is exactly when she must take active steps forward. *What do I need to do next?* is her new mantra, compared to the global *Nothing will help* motto she first brought with her. (For the record, I state here globally that I have never worn sandals with socks.)

GLOBALLY POSITIVE?

But wait, you might be thinking, *aren't some people globally positive?*

Everything's coming up roses!

All's well that ends well!

Even Mother Teresa made global statements: "Spread love everywhere you go. Let no one ever come to you without leaving happier."

Globally positive people don't come into my office very often looking for help. They're focusing on the good things! But even striving to be globally positive has its drawbacks. I've recently started hearing and talking more about the pitfalls of toxic positivity. For example, if a teen has just been rejected in some way and the well-meaning adults work to convince her that "It's all for the best" and she "shouldn't feel badly," they may be sending the message that there's no room for sadness or other negative emotions, that all experiences must have a silver lining. Ask a grieving person what it's like to come up against global positivity: "He's in a better place now," or, "At least you had her, even if the time was short," or, "She wouldn't want you to be sad!" The best of intentions come across as dismissive or insensitive.

I do concede that being globally positive is likely less harmful in the long run, but being global on either end of the spectrum gets in the way of handling a range of experiences and emotions and relationships. Being flexible and nuanced as you move through life's challenges is key to solid emotional health and connection with others. A global style impacts how you see the world, how you see yourself and others, and perhaps most significantly, how you solve problems and handle challenges. Ironically, global thinking is everywhere, so let's break it down.

VIEWING YOUR WORLD GLOBALLY

Because anxiety seeks certainty, the lure of seeing your world in global, black-and-white terms is compelling to the anxious part of you. If all dogs bite and you stay away from all dogs, you are safe. If you see all bridges as collapses waiting to happen or all planes as flying death traps, avoiding them lessens your odds of disaster. In this way, being global feels good. These broad categories give your life operating rules. You work to remove ambiguity and uncertainty and risk. You feel protected and comfortable. Or do you?

If you're a worrier, your global perceptions also fuel your negative, scary, catastrophic narratives. Anxiety that goes global takes something small and makes it big. Accuracy isn't all that important. Worrying takes one piece of information and makes it a broad truth, even if that piece of information is false—and that's the problem. Global is often big, scary—and wrong.

A good example is the "stranger danger" programs that popped up in the 1980s. These initiatives, designed to protect children from victimization, became standard. And even though stranger abductions, particularly of young children, are incredibly rare and have remained so for decades, school programs and television programs and milk cartons made it feel ubiquitous. Notably, when the concept of stranger danger was widely introduced, children were told that all strangers were dangerous *even if they looked nice*. Even more notable? Over the last several decades, the effectiveness of many informational programs designed to prevent abduction is close to zero. The programs do not teach skills that work.

This is an example of global thinking. It distorts our perception of the risk of stranger abduction, but perhaps more importantly it globally "teaches" children that all strangers are dangerous. When my young boys and I were separated at an amusement park, they went to a security guard at the entrance because I had taught them to look for someone wearing a name tag or uniform. (Some parents tell their children to seek out another mom with children, also a helpful distinction.) In that park, my boys were surrounded by strangers, and I'm sure most would have helped. What if I had taught them that all strangers are dangerous? What if I believed that as well? How many times have you benefitted from the kindness of strangers?

If you are anxious and lean toward the catastrophic, your danger-infused global view will also support avoidance. There are experiences you will never have, places you will always avoid, people you will never meet, and jobs you won't pursue. You will apply these avoidant strategies globally without assessing the different factors involved.

With one family who came to see me for a consultation, I immediately noticed that the two daughters sat with the posture of ballet dancers on the very edge of the couch. I didn't say anything at first, but since we were working on the family's pattern of rigidity around some significant phobias, I asked about their posture several minutes into the appointment. "Lice is everywhere," one of the girls said. "We never sit back on any cloth furniture." I questioned how they went to school or the movies or a friend's house. How did they determine if the lice risk was high or low? It was just better to take no chances, they said, as their mother nodded in agreement.

An acquaintance of mine had food poisoning following dinner at a local restaurant. I understand not going back to that restaurant; the memory of being sick and the idea that this restaurant was lax with food safety made it an unappetizing option. But this person vowed never to eat in a restaurant again. *Ever.*

Someone told me once they would never go hiking in the mountains because of bears. Bears? Many areas of the world have mountains and *no bears*. And many bears in the woods want nothing to do with humans. If you live in New England like me, and really want to avoid bears, you can hike in the winter while the bears are hibernating. (But be prepared for freezing temperatures, far more likely to kill you than a bear.) Are there some parts of the country where bears are a potential danger? Certainly. I've hiked there, and it was risky. We had to make some decisions based on information we received; for example, a mama grizzly and her two cubs were spotted in one area, so we chose a different hike.

People do get lice and food poisoning. Bears sometimes threaten or maul hikers. Bad things happen, so becoming less globally anxious about the world doesn't mean you now ignore all risk. It pays to be global *sometimes.* (I can confidently and globally announce that I will never approach a mama grizzly bear that is protecting her cubs.) But to shift out of a global stance, you must work to consider the context, stay open to information, and adjust as needed. Not all strangers are dangerous. Some restaurants will make you ill, but many won't.

If you are global, how do you make those distinctions?

UN-GLOBALLY YOU

Growing up, were you seen as the smart one, the athletic one, the shy one, or the loud one? Were you described as the smaller version of one of your parents, what we refer to now as a "mini-me"? Honestly, I cringe a bit when I hear parents describe their children in such global terms. The artist. The rebel. The angel. People change and grow, yet I see children, teens, and adults locked into these roles, these perceptions of themselves. The baby of the family. The responsible one. The brat.

If you were shy as a kid, that doesn't mean you'll be for your whole life. Alcoholics get sober. Couch potatoes decide to run marathons, and triathletes become sedentary. You may have a sarcastic sense of humor with your close friends but choose to tuck that part of yourself away when you, the teacher, walk into your first-grade classroom and greet your students. You may have strong political beliefs but decide to be less vocal about them when visiting your grandfather. You are not one thing, nor are you destined to stay the same through your entire existence. *Keeping you stuck* is anxiety's superpower, so being globally wed to an all-or-nothing, overgeneralized view of you just won't do.

Sadly, I think this trend of defining ourselves and others in global terms is becoming more pervasive and intense. For over thirty years, I have been in a profession that supposedly exists to help people change and grow and recover. But over the last decade, more and more language supports a global and often permanent definition of anxiety and depression that counteracts that mission. And it's coming from the profession itself—not all of us, but enough of us. Instead of focusing on the skills and connections that enable people to change reactions and form new pathways in the brain (neuroplasticity), many now refer to anxiety and depression as diseases and disabilities. Though anxiety can clearly be disabling, globally defining oneself as permanently anxious and then living one's life based on this global definition has been harmful, not helpful.

Just as you may globally conclude that all dogs bite, you may also conclude that you are "just an anxious person." When you view your anxiety as a permanent, dominating fixture in your personality rather than an occasional flare-up of a *part of who you are*, you act accordingly. Others do, too. You meet those expectations. When I speak to high school and college students, I often say, "It's important for you to learn about you because there are things you do that make anxiety and depression worse, and there are things you can learn and do to make it better. You need to learn about your operating system so that you can adjust as you grow, reduce your risk factors, and develop those skills."

When I first started saying this directly, I was surprised at how consistently some students became angry with me. I was even booed! I thought I was offering them a helpful and optimistic message about managing their well-being. What I was doing, they said, was blaming them for who they were.

"I have a disability!" one young woman yelled at me. "It's who I am, and the goal is for me and everyone else to accept that!"

What a shame. The global pattern was already in place, and it wasn't her doing. This is what she had been told. And since she now globally accepted this view of herself, any conflicting point of view was vehemently rejected. She would fight for this identity. It was her self-concept and probably still is.

If you see yourself as globally anxious—if you see your anxiety as a big, unchangeable part of you—then you will do the very things that make it worse. You will put this part of you in charge. You will seek certainty. You will avoid. You'll stay put, which is right where your worries prefer you to stay: put.

This pattern might impact you in seemingly minor ways. You'll never fly in a plane, so you won't see other parts of the world and won't attend your cousin's wedding in Puerto Rico. *Big deal*, you tell yourself. You always avoid crowds, so you stand in the back at your daughter's recital or graduation. You can still see her up there. Your family understands this is *who you are*, so they cooperate and adjust to your rules. Until they can't or won't.

An acquaintance I'll call Sharon routinely described herself as "an anxious mess." "Everyone knows I can't handle stress, so we work around it," she told me. "For example, there's no way I'd ever drive on the highway, so don't even suggest it." Then her daughter—no longer willing to "work around it"—moved several states away with her new husband. When she became pregnant soon after, the daughter hoped Sharon would come to help after the baby was born. Sharon was livid. How was she going to get there? How could her daughter even ask such a thing? Her daughter was making her feel guilty! "I don't drive on the highway, period," she said. "She knows that will never change."

Trauma expert Lisa Ferentz wrote an article in 2016 describing her evolution from a new therapist trained to focus on the pathology of trauma to a skilled therapist who recognized the power of our many parts: the hurtful ones and the strong ones, the destructive ones and the creative ones. About her training in the 1980s, Lisa writes, "Little, if any, attention was paid to the inner strengths that traumatized clients might reclaim if given half a chance. With the focus all on pathology, all the time, it was no wonder therapists tended to regard clients as one-dimensional bundles of dysfunction and pain." (Note to reader: selecting therapists who specialize in active, strengths-based therapy is very important if you're seeking counseling.)

Lisa began to realize that her clients' most upsetting behaviors—the products of their trauma—were survival strategies, and creative ones at that. Brilliantly and compassionately, she started to help her clients recognize the traumatized parts *and* the parts of them that were looking to heal and flourish. She wanted people to acknowledge their trauma but not define themselves by it. When Lisa discovered positive psychology, a framework introduced by Martin Seligman in the late 1970s, and the concept of posttraumatic growth (PTG) developed by psychologists Lawrence Calhoun and Richard Tedeschi, she shifted away from that global and often pathologizing approach—an approach that I unfortunately was also trained in and learned—to a more flexible and strengths-based perspective. She viewed her traumatized clients as a collection of *many parts*—painful and inspiring—and helped them see themselves through that same lens. Using the metaphor of an orchestra, Lisa writes, "For me, the notion of conducting a kind of therapeutic symphony began to resonate more and more. I saw my clients' multifaceted experiences, thoughts, and emotions as components of an orchestra."

Many anxious people have experienced trauma. Sixty to seventy percent of anxious people will also struggle with depression—and all of us have experienced some worry, fear, and grief in our childhoods or adult lives. This is not at all about denying or minimizing the struggle. In fact, finding someone to help you untangle your experiences and recognize your many parts may be necessary to move you out of your global framework. There are no experiences, minor or major, where identifying yourself globally as anxious, afraid, or damaged is either accurate or helpful. You are not one thing. You are a symphony—a symphony full of beautiful passages, wrong notes, missed cues, and countless other human imperfections.

WITH PERFECTIONISM, IT'S BEST OR BUST!

Perfectionism is the ultimate global, all-or-nothing stance. Its impact is far-reaching. If you don't score perfectly, then you failed. If you don't win every match, you're a loser. If your boss gives you negative feedback on a project or asks you to revise a part of it, you're a complete idiot. This type of black-or-white thinking is jet fuel for anxiety's demand for certainty. Global expectations of yourself or others leave no room for mistakes, no room for embarrassment, and no room for repair or recovery.

This type of thinking is hard to miss. Big messages extolling the virtue of *being your best* are everywhere. On the surface they're appealing and meant to be inspiring.

Strive for perfection in everything you do!

Nothing but the best!

When you work your hardest, anything is possible!

And do you remember this popular daily affirmation?

Every day in every way, I'm getting better and better.

Wowza.

Our culture rewards perfectionism. We love a winner, someone who beats the odds and pushes harder than anyone else to win the race. The focus on being the best is equated with fame and riches and adoration. There is no room for error. Success is often measured with the yardstick of perfectionism based on what we see on the outside. Undeniably, as spectators, we enjoy watching the external results of a perfectionistic drive. I count myself among those easily pulled in, captivated by the story.

Despite the high emotional and physical costs to the participants, we as observers applaud and admire the many arenas where success and perfectionism look to be one and the same. Perfectionism can create the appearance of success. It's hard to acknowledge how this type of rigid, all-or-nothing approach creates anxiety, depression, and physical injury, but it's right there. Watch Olympic gymnastics if you need a clear example of perfectionism and the pressure of an all-or-nothing mentality. One small misstep takes an athlete out of contention. One bobble on the beam knocks them off the medal podium. It's so suspenseful! Amazing! But these young people have loudly sounded the alarm if we choose to pay attention. The cost of this perfectionistic culture is high, they tell us. While we get caught up in the heavily commercialized narrative of hard work paying off, they talk about injury, eating disorders, anxiety, depression, and concealed, denied long-term abuse.

The 2021 documentary *Weight of Gold* featuring Michael Phelps goes straight at the issue of perfectionism, mental health, and the pressure of Olympic athletes to achieve one thing: a gold medal. The documentary profiles athletes who met expectations, like Phelps and speed skater Apolo Ohno, and also shines a light on those who fell short, like track star Lolo Jones, who hit a hurdle when she was seconds from capturing gold, and skier Bode Miller, the odds-on favorite who shocked the world and was vilified by the media when he came home without a single medal. Regardless of medal success or failure, Olympic athletes spoke of the all-or-nothing lives they led and the emotional crash they experienced when this singular identity was gone. Depression, they explained, is the expected outcome—a large and unspoken part of the process of pursuing gold.

Sasha Cohen, the twenty-two-year-old American figure skater who fell during her 2006 Olympic long program and settled for silver, found the pressure to succeed and the experience of coming up short overwhelming. Working to understand the crest of her Olympic pursuit, she says, "We are Olympic athletes and we're not sure if we're anything else." Phelps ends the documentary with an observation that all global perfectionists can understand, even those who are not Olympic record holders: "When you've devoted your life to a pursuit of such a singular goal and then leave it all behind . . . there's that giant question: Now what? And even bigger? Who am I?"

These examples are extreme, but I also see perfectionism play out in the day-to-day lives of parents and children. The cost is equally significant. The belief that you must do things perfectly or that things aren't worth doing unless you "always give it your all" is exhausting and unrealistic. And the pressure to succeed is there, regardless of whether you fail privately or your story is played out for all the world to see.

I'll never forget talking to a mother of two young girls who came up to me after a community presentation. She was a physician, she told me, and had worked incredibly hard to achieve her goals. Her parents were immigrants who wanted their children to succeed. Being the best, she said, was a value that her own family embraced, and it paid off. What was bothering her right now, she said, leaning in and speaking softly, was the impact this approach might have on her parenting. She could already feel the anxiety inside her when her girls didn't "push themselves" or when they didn't want to participate in an activity. If her second-grader missed a word on a spelling test or made an error on a math worksheet, they sat together until her daughter, often through tears, *got it right*.

"After they go to bed at night, I stay up making sure the house is perfectly picked up," she said. And she recently started arranging the furniture and little figures in the girls' dollhouse so they would play out scenarios she thought valuable. Every moment was a teachable moment, she said, and this approach to parenting reverberated all around her. No opportunity was to be wasted.

"I am anxious all the time. I have pressure at my job. I'm expected to be perfect. And I want to be a perfect mom. I think I want my daughters to be perfect, too, but you're telling me that'll screw them up."

Standing there in an auditorium at nine in the evening among a crowd of people, I couldn't solve her issue. But even in that five-minute exchange, I could gently point out the rigidity and fear that propelled her perfectionistic, global style. She was not imagining it. If she didn't make all A's as a student, she wouldn't be admitted into the next top program. Once she became a doctor, any mistake would put lives and her career in jeopardy. The competition and expectations were intense. So if she allowed her daughters to be quitters now, how would they learn to be successful later? Any slip would lead to global failure.

She lived her life intensely, as if she were constantly performing a balance-beam routine at the Olympics.

As I've said, changing this requires a more nuanced approach, one that allows for flexibility and adjustment. For some, like this successful woman, it means allowing for a more balanced assessment of herself and her achievements. She's certainly made mistakes and survived. And there's no way she's been a perfect parent, nor have her girls been even close to perfect little humans! She loves and nurtures her daughters; as a family they screw up, and the world keeps turning. But does she ignore or discount these experiences? Has she learned to equate flexibility with failure? I'd bet on it. She anticipates disaster, imagines worst-case scenarios, and loses sleep. "One wrong move" is the looming adage. It all feels so *dangerous*. Global thinking and catastrophic thinking know each other very, very well. I hope you're seeing how these sneaky patterns join together, and how that increases their grip.

GLOBAL LABELS IN LOVE

Many of the examples of global reactions in this chapter have something in common: the impact on relationships. Sharon missed out on her grandchild's birth and was resentful of her daughter's decision to move. The perfectionistic physician parented with more fear than fun. Middle-schooler Lucia was withdrawing from her social world at a time developmentally when social connection was essential to her well-being.

Global thinking in relationships isn't different from global thinking anywhere else. Remember, the goal of this book is to help you recognize the larger processes and patterns, rather than get tangled up in the specifics of the content. But I want to bring up global thinking and relationships specifically because global thinking and clichés about relationships are common in our culture and quite prevalent in the world of therapy and self-help. The cost of accepting these global statements about relationships as truisms is high.

Acclaimed marriage therapist and bestselling author Michele Weiner-Davis has spent her career pushing back against "accepted" global beliefs about relationships, divorce, and infidelity. Acutely aware of the cost, she challenges therapists and couples to move away from these sweeping reactions, labels, and assumptions. Her focus is squarely on what's possible in a given relationship and the actions needed to change patterns. I asked her for a list of the most pervasive and often destructive global beliefs she encounters. Here's what she shared:

If you loved me, you would know what I need from you.

If our marriage were a good one, the same things would be important to us.

If you have to work hard on your marriage, it means it's flawed.

You can't bring back "in love" feelings.

People don't change.

Once a cheat, always a cheat.

And I'll add my favorite from the iconic 1970 film *Love Story* with Ryan O'Neal and Ali McGraw:

"Love means never having to say you're sorry."

Global thinking and its inherent rigidity impair and destroy relationships. Jumping to conclusions and labeling people ruin marriages, divide family members, and end friendships. This is not to say that every marriage should be saved or that every family member should be embraced. We do not counterbalance global in one direction with global in the opposite direction. But the goal in many cases is to question the broad and unchallenged perceptions that cut you off from others. The collateral damage of such a stance is huge—namely because it intensifies *the pattern of inner isolation*, a pattern so amplified by the pandemic, social media, and our current state of divisiveness that I devote the entire next chapter to it.

WHAT TO DO

Global Language Alert

Listening for global language as we go through everyday routines is a game I play with my clients. If you have children, it's a great way to increase everyone's awareness in a playful way.

Kids use global language when they're frustrated: "You *never* let us have fun!" "My teacher *always* gives me the hard assignments!"

Parents do, too: "You are *always* on that phone."

One anxious mom said to her daughter in my office, "I will *never* let anything happen to you! Do you understand? *Never!*"

Listen to advertisements designed to make you feel better by pointing out that we all have the same issues and are thus globally in need of the same solution. You're just like everyone else: inadequate and in need of a fix. A radio ad in the Boston area makes me chuckle whenever I hear it. The ad is for a guy named Big Lou who sells life insurance. His radio adds starts with the declaration: "Diabetes meds, high blood pressure meds, anxiety meds . . . everyone's on them!"

His tagline: "Call Big Lou. He's like you. He's on meds, too!" The odds are in his favor, but I think it's a bit of a global presumption.

And how about romantic comedies and iconic songs? (I apologize in advance for ruining your future listening.) "You were always on my mind," sang Willie Nelson. "I will always love you," wrote Dolly Parton. "Nobody does it better," crooned Carly Simon in a 1977 James Bond theme song. Kudos to the Rolling Stones for standing out as an exception: "You can't always get what you want, / but if you try sometimes, / you just might find, / you get what you need." How unglobal of them.

Pay attention to when and where you hear those global words. At your job? In your family? From the meteorologist? How quickly do you buy into and believe the global attributions of others? How likely are you to use global language? (If nothing else, by paying attention to this language, you will be less prone to fall prey to advertisers' assertions.)

And if you deplore this attribute in others—it fuels bigotry, for example—it's important to notice how often *you* direct global criticism in your own direction. What conclusions have you reached about you? What do you offhandedly say about your abilities? How do your global statements and beliefs about you keep you stuck, in small and big ways?

Think and Act the Part of Parts

Now that you are paying attention and hearing global language all around you, working to think and respond *with a parts mindset* that logically steps to the front of the line. Recognizing how much of your life's experiences is made up of parts—you, other people, tasks—is the opposite of being global. While global wants to go big and hang out with its pal catastrophic thinking, parts thinking helps us slow down and break it down, offering us perspective and helpful distance.

Parts thinking came up earlier. We externalized the repetitive negative thinking part in chapter 1 by giving it a name and observing its predicable patterns. Lisa Ferentz described the importance of recognizing and valuing different parts of people as she helps them shift their posttrauma view. I often tell parents to think of parenting as a series of chapters, with different headings and skills needed along the way. This also applies to marriages and careers.

Interrupt Global Reactions (Imperfectly)

As you shift toward a parts frame of mind, you must continually work to interrupt global reactions and global anticipation, and to embrace the value of sequencing and compartmentalization. These are concrete skills that you can develop. You will improve, but you will not do it perfectly because your emotions—your normal, human emotions—will also respond and at times work against you.

In circumstances when you are overwhelmed, the skill of recognizing parts often disappears. When you're furious or scared, stepping back and looking at the different aspects of the situation is not going to happen, which is normal and expected. During this initial reaction, the more sophisticated parts of your brain are unavailable; the emotional and survival parts take charge. These parts together are called the limbic system, and the key areas in this reactive system of our brains are the hippocampus, the amygdala, and the hypothalamus. These parts of the brain quickly evaluate and respond on an unconscious level in a system designed to keep us safe. But this system is not always accurate, as we learned with catastrophic thinking.

The longer-term goal, then, is to move out of global thinking as soon as possible and to make sure the global response does not go unquestioned over time, thus allowing it to become more permanent and generalized.

And know this: None of us gets through life completely free of global reactions. It's even normal in certain circumstances to find yourself in both places at once, or to move back and forth between global, overwhelming thoughts and parts thinking. The goal is to extricate yourself from that very rigid global place as quickly as you can.

When I lost my sons at the amusement park, I had a moment of pure panic. I turned around, and my children were not there. I was the sole adult in charge, and they were *gone*. I remember frantically scanning the area, retracing my steps, and calling for them. During those first moments, everything happening inside me felt *big*: big pounding heart rate, big eyes, big voice, big fears, big imagination. And that park was big. (The only thing that was small, I soon found out—other than my rather small boys—was the number of security staff on duty: two young men. "We're cutting back on our shifts," said the one I finally located.) But staying in that big, global, overwhelmed place would not do. I needed to think *Parts*. What steps did I need to take? I became methodical. I went to the courtesy booth. "They will be brought here," the person told me.

I checked our meeting spot. I went back to the booth. Checked the front gate and back to the booth. It took over an hour, but then there they were. They had also come up with a plan, they told me. "We figured kids get lost here a lot," they said. They looked for me for a few minutes and then decided to go to the meeting spot. (I had gone to the wrong one, as it turns out.) When I didn't show up, they went to the front gate. They asked for help and were brought to the courtesy booth. Steps. We were all worried, yet we did not "go global," at least not for long and not permanently. But make no mistake, we had our moments. We are imperfect humans—as underscored by me going to the wrong meeting place!

You, like me, will screw up and go global. Changing this pattern, as with all of them, is about adjusting. I don't want you to ruminate about your tendency to ruminate, or to catastrophize how your catastrophizing has impacted your kids, or to globalize about being global by telling yourself that you will *never go global again*.

Instead, it's a consistent diet of gently correcting yourself and showing your family how that sounds. If you go global and, in a moment of frustration, yell, "You kids *never* help out around the house!" you can then stop yourself and say, "Okay, sorry, let me back up. That was a global statement. Last week, you guys were super-helpful. Today, you're driving me crazy because I've asked you five times to pick up the crap all over the house and you haven't done it."

People often tell me that they understand intellectually what I'm saying, and it makes good sense. It's just hard in the moment. Yup, it is. That's why it's truly okay, and I encourage to do that postgame analysis. If you dump some global goo on your family or partner, come back later and say, "Did you hear that global stuff coming out of me? Let me try that again." When you step back and own it, you're modeling flexibility and self-awareness and decreasing resentment. As always, give yourself time and space and room for error. Even Mother Teresa used global language.

And love actually *does* mean saying you're sorry. A lot.

Compartmentalize

Compartmentalizing is the ability to contain one part of you or an experience while you deal with something else. You say to yourself, *I need to put this part into a separate box for a while so that I can focus on this other thing*. When you're on a tight deadline for a work project, you may need to put aside the conflict you're having with a family member to better focus on the task. When you are spending time with your teenager, you need to separate from your work stress to stay connected and attentive to her. During the pandemic, the compartments that many depended upon disappeared. Feeling overwhelmed and anxious was a common result. Parents were trying to work and supervise toddlers at the same time. Teens who had competently managed their own schoolwork now had parents listening in (and commenting) on every Zoom class. All my therapy sessions were done on video, of course, and many people were eager to come back to my office in person because they wanted the separation, the compartment of my office.

Compartments in our lives can help: a defined place to work or study, or time constraints and clear expectations about what needs to get done and who needs to be where. With anxious people, however, I often find that even when external compartments are in place, the internal ability to compartmentalize is not there. Does this sound familiar? In chapter 1, I described the trap of overthinking. We are seduced by the idea that more thought is better thought. If you tend to go global, work on consciously giving yourself permission to problem solve, then unhook from the global statements of doom that overwhelm you. *I have to complete this project, so let me put some deadlines in place and start chipping away at it* sounds and feels different than the global *I'll never be able to organize this entire house!*

Compartmentalization also allows you to handle an anticipated or repeated stressful situation without permitting it to invade and hijack your whole life. This is helpful when you must do something you already know will be unpleasant. Say, for example, you hate going to the dentist but you responsibly schedule your annual cleanings. You've already succeeded by compartmentalizing your distaste for the dentist in service to your dental health. You're choosing action over avoidance. You're going. So now that you've decided on your plan, how will global announcements and negatively anticipating your dentist appointment do any good? They won't.

> I absolutely dread going to the dentist! It's the worst!
>
> Every time I brush my teeth, I obsess about my dentist appointment (which could be eight or ten months away)!
>
> I never like going. . . . I always think they're going to find something wrong.

If your teeth are generally healthy, you'll spend less than two hours a year at the dentist, and yet your global thoughts about the appointment hijack you on a regular basis. You have a habitual, dread-filled response about going to the dentist, and you indulge it almost daily. The dentist isn't the problem. The global thinking is.

How can you engage in more balanced thinking about the dentist? What does that sound like?

Notice the containment in the following phrases, how a shift in language puts a dentist visit realistically in its proper place (once a year for an hour):

> I really like my dentist, but I honestly don't enjoy the forty minutes of scraping.
>
> Luckily my teeth are healthy. Funny how going to the dentist helps me from having to go to the dentist.
>
> When I'm in the dentist chair twice a year, I'm in the chair. There's no need to rehearse being at the dentist when I'm actually not at the dentist because I do handle being at the dentist.

Fiona, a teen with a medical condition, must receive an injection once a week, done at home by her parents each Tuesday night. When she first began receiving the shots, she thought about them all the time. The shot itself took five minutes, but she globally anticipated and focused on it the other six days a week. There was some relief from her worry on Tuesday night and into Wednesday, but it was fleeting. Our goal was to make the routine smaller, not bigger—to contain the experience of the shot to the actual experience of the shot, rather than have the jab and the medical condition that required it globally define her.

Fiona needed a shift in how she handled her thinking about the injection, a new script. With practice, she was able to notice her global language around the weekly event and how much longer and more painful her anticipation was compared to the actual procedure. Getting the injection is now redefined as one part of her happily full life. The injection occurs on just one part of her very amazing self. Part, not whole. A bit painful, but contained and quick. She and her parents work together to do what needs to be done, when it needs to be done, minus the previously overwhelming (and free-range) discussion, anticipation, and reaction. By using this skill of compartmentalization, the lousy parts of the experience no longer globally contaminate huge chunks of time or ruin entire days talking and thinking about the shot.

One last reminder: As with all these skills, don't go too far in the other direction and compartmentalize in too global or rigid a way. Being able to get some distance and put something away for a while is great, but if you start to compartmentalize globally (*I'll never think about that again* or *I'll never let myself feel sad like that*), then you are cutting off a part of yourself. If Fiona's goal was to not think about the injection, not feel the injection at all, and pretend the injection didn't exist, we wouldn't have made such great progress. Elimination strategies don't work. The worry is going to be there. Expect it, allow it, and respond differently when it arrives.

Sequencing: Putting the Horse in Front of the Cart Matters

Sequencing is used to break down an event or task into simple steps and then *put those steps in order*. It's often taught by speech-language pathologists to help children communicate events and stories clearly, with a beginning, middle, and end. Additionally, children with executive functioning issues often have trouble with sequencing. They hear the instructions but can't process and organize them in a way needed to complete the task. Adults get frustrated at the child's unwillingness to follow directions, but that's not truly what's going on if you have trouble with sequencing. Not knowing how to order your day and tasks impacts the ability to identify problems and solutions. It can disrupt social interactions and create frustrating family dynamics.

Sequencing skills also fall apart when anxiety takes control. For our purposes, sequencing is a "parts" skill that combats anxiety's creation of global, overwhelming confusion. Knowing what steps to take and when to take them sounds obvious, but when you are immersed in all-or-nothing thinking or viewing a problem through a global lens, it's easy to lose track of that skill. How often have you stood in front of a disorganized closet, a flooded basement, or a pile of bills and said to yourself, *I have no idea where to start.*

Perhaps you're tackling something new. You want to remove wallpaper or apply for a new health insurance plan or crate-train a puppy, but it's daunting. You feel that familiar uncertainty and doubt, saying to yourself, *This is impossible to figure out.* I remember learning how to drive a stick-shift car. That's a very sequential skill. You shift in order from one gear to the next. But as soon as I hit traffic or had to get going on a hill, the logical order of a manual transmission and the steps I needed to follow disappeared from my brain, often in a fog of anxiety and panic.

Or what if you repeatedly find yourself in the same frustrating situation and are confused as to why? You complain to your friends (and they complain to each other about you), "How does this keep happening over and over again?" When I ask anxious, global thinkers how to tackle a task or solve a problem, their vague responses often reveal a long-term pattern of global avoidance that makes it impossible to learn the sequence, to experiment with the trial-and-error process of the steps along the way. When something scares, intimidates, or overwhelms global thinkers, they keep a distance. They avoid, never getting past the first step nor allowing their skills and confidence to build. Or they rush and jump into the middle, just to get it over with, without recognizing the value of taking it step by step.

To shake up your global patterns and improve your use of parts and sequencing, start here:

- *Expect those overwhelming thoughts and feelings to show up at the start or along the way of a new or challenging project.* The more experience you have, the better you get at managing the challenging task, but those thoughts and feelings don't completely go away. Whenever I sit down to start an article or a chapter of a book or a new workshop, I feel overwhelmed. In fact, between you and me, I call it the "cry feeling," and it hits me between the eyes. When I began this very book, I texted my dear friend and college roommate Karen, an acclaimed fiction writer: "Can you just tell me that starting a book is really hard and that I will finish by April?"

"Starting a book is really hard and you will finish it by April," she responded. And then she wrote this:

> Do you know the Annie Lamott story about starting a project? Her brother had put off a report on birds 'til the last

> minute. He's sitting at the dining room table, books spread all around him, in despair. His dad passes, pats his head, and says, "Bird by bird, buddy, take it bird by bird."

Which leads me directly to my next tip.

- *Have a mantra, a little reminder that pulls you out of global overreaction and puts you back into steps and parts.* "Bird by bird" has worked well for me. Twelve-step programs recognize the danger of global thinking and the value of simple slogans that shift awareness and break things down. Some popular "sequence" slogans include "One Day at a Time," "First Things First," and "Progress, Not Perfection." I suggest writing these phrases down on index cards or sticky notes and putting them in places where you will see them frequently. Over time, they become more automatic when you feel overwhelmed. They offer a short, alternative burst to weaken your global announcements.
- *Ask for help and observe others who already know the steps and the sequence of what you're tackling.* This sounds obvious, but many of us don't do it. When people are trying to change their diet, health coaches give them a grocery list and instructions on how to prepare for the inevitable hunger and cravings that will strike. If I'm going to fit in a trip to the gym before my workday starts, I need to concretely think about the steps involved to determine when I'll leave the house, what I'll do when there, and when I'll arrive back home. If I don't pay attention to the sequence, I will screw up my schedule, and my day will become immediately more stressful.
- *Use visuals like checklists and outlines to help you break down the task and follow a sequence.* Again, sounds obvious, but I talk to many people—particularly teens—who do not write

down a plan or a schedule. If you've never done this and tend to feel disorganized and overwhelmed as you move through life, you may need help with your executive functioning skills. It's not too late to get some coaching. Someone out there knows how to do it and how to teach it. Ask.

The Thrill of Cutting Corners

If your global, all-or-nothing thinking has resulted in perfectionism, you likely don't have trouble with sequencing or organization. But you do have trouble knowing when and where to cut corners, and I cannot more enthusiastically endorse this skill as a way to shift your thinking and behavior. As I said earlier, the idea of being perfect and doing our best is so ingrained that when I even *suggest* to perfectionists the idea of coasting or cutting corners, I'm met with snorts and sometimes anger. I am not suggesting that you stop succeeding, challenging yourself, working hard, or achieving—but I am suggesting that you question the message and the consequences of this "best" mindset, especially if as a parent you are seeing it in your children.

More perfectionism doesn't get you out of the trap of perfectionism. Perfectionists don't ultimately arrive one day at that perfect destination of peace and satisfaction. Any "perfect" result is quickly eclipsed in the present by the fear of a future failure. H. Jackson Brown Jr., author of the 1991 bestselling self-help volume *Life's Little Instruction Book*, wrote, "If you're doing your best, you won't have any time to worry about failure." I strongly disagree. I believe quite the opposite is true. Those trapped in "best" worry a boatload about failure. Just ask Bill Belichick, coach of the New England Patriots. Upon winning yet another Super Bowl, he was already lamenting how far behind he was organizing next year's team.

So how do you make this shift? First, externalize that perfectionist, black-or-white part of you and hear what it consistently says. Where do those messages come from? How does your perfectionism motivate you? Is it fear? Do you know the difference between what is actually needed or desired, and what your internal voice is demanding? What is it like inside of you when you make a mistake? Have you ever decided not to listen?

Then play around with the skill of cutting corners. Start by giving yourself permission to find an easier way in a few areas of your life. Give yourself some room to experiment, disregarding or toying with the rules that perfectionism put into place, even without your consent. Where can you coast? It's decidedly *not* all-or-nothing, so see where there's wiggle room. Perhaps the physician mom I described earlier can start by allowing her children to play without her direction and control. She then models flexibility to her daughters even as she realistically continues to feel the pressure of her career.

Several years ago, I heard Martha Stewart describe how she solves the entertaining problem of ensuring all the food on her menu is ready to serve at the same time. Her solution astounded me. Paraphrasing her, she said, "I only have one main dish that needs to be cooked and served hot. Everything else is made ahead and is served chilled or at room temperature." What? Martha Stewart, as skilled at entertaining as anyone on the planet, keeps it simple, cutting some corners? Brilliant.

How and where can you cut some corners? Where can you give yourself permission to coast? How can you back away from those global, all-or-nothing rules that define you, and maybe even take some of those rules a little less seriously? And who will be grateful for the change?

QUESTIONS FOR PONDERING AND JOURNALING
When do you tend to be the most global?
Who around you tends to fall into this pattern? How does that impact you?
Write out the conversation you will have with your family about shifting out of globally negative language and *how* you will work together to change the pattern.
If you hold global beliefs that are based in fear or anxiety, ask yourself: *What happens when I obey this global belief? What happens if I loosen this global, rigid belief? What's the risk in keeping my options open?*

CHAPTER FOUR

INNER ISOLATION AND DISCONNECTION

Sneaky Pattern: How Anxiety's Fear of Judgment Isolates and Disconnects Us from People

Perhaps the secret of living well is not in having all the answers but in pursuing unanswerable questions in good company.

—Rachel Naomi Remen

My friend Adam describes himself as 75 percent introverted. He has no problem going to see a movie or concert alone. He's happy for company if he's going on a hike, but equally pleased to spend a day by himself going up and down a mountain. He is warm and funny, but until you know him well, he won't share too much about himself. When he's around larger groups of people, he listens more than he talks. Professionally, he interacts with people all the time; in fact, his profession requires it. He combines social agility with clear boundaries. People enjoy his company, and he has many friends from many areas of his life, even though people would likely describe him as shy or quiet.

In contrast, I had a friend Darcy for a brief time when I was a young adult. She was also introverted, but unlike Adam, her relationships were often disappointing to her. Socially, Darcy struggled. I know she longed for connection because we talked about it. She didn't have many close friends growing up, she told me, and she knew it was because she was shy and very anxious. Sometimes she blamed others for not giving her a chance or blamed the culture for its standards of extroversion. But most often, she went inside herself, trying to figure out on her own why she felt so disconnected. She was lonely and carried great shame. I tried to help, but I don't think I did. Honestly, she truly was hard to connect with, and back then I didn't have a clue how to even address that in a way that felt caring. I didn't know what to do, so I did nothing.

Now I know better. If Darcy were to show up in my office as a client (and many with her same struggles do), I would explain how her internal ruminations only increase her isolation. I would coach her on the dance we must do between boundaries and social risk. We would talk concretely about how her anxious patterns predictably get in her way and what to do about them. But we met under different circumstances. She was a friend, not a client. And when I moved away, I left behind the heavy awkwardness of that tenuous friendship. All these years later, I believe this to be true: I was added to her list, another person who compounded her belief that she couldn't and wouldn't have close friendships.

As we tackle this next pattern of inner isolation and disconnection, Adam and Darcy illustrate a distinction, one that the pandemic didn't create but exacerbated: isolation can be situational or perceptual. Although I'd describe both Adam and Darcy as introverted and quiet, Adam did fine emotionally during the pandemic. He had times of loneliness, but he also had a variety of social connections coupled with the ability to maintain them. Rates of reported anxiety and depression increased, but those like Adam who identified their loneliness during the height of the pandemic as situational did better. Recognizing the isolation as a collective and shared experience most certainly helped many get through it. "We're in this together" became the chant. We may have been lonely, but if we recognized we weren't alone in that loneliness, we fared better. There was connection.

But for those like Darcy who struggled with connection, alone became brutally lonelier. During the lockdown, the pain of inner disconnection felt all too familiar. The pandemic made things worse, for sure, but it was not the original source. Darcy's pattern was primarily perceptual and fueled by a pattern of anxiety and a sense of *not belonging*. Disconnection did not arrive with Covid—but the pandemic, complicated by the social, racial, and political discord we have faced, has put a spotlight upon it. Existing emotional cracks have widened into chasms, and recovery from these wounds has been slow, impacting all age groups but especially teens and young adults.

I have talked to so many who, before, during, and after the pandemic, describe a feeling of being on the outside. They know there's a club they wish to join but are unable to figure out the secrets of membership. Brilliant couples therapist and author Esther Perel said it beautifully when describing what she encounters in her practice: "Sometimes I have some of that sense in my [therapy] room. People come, and I'm thinking, it's not what they're experiencing. It's the fact that they're experiencing it completely alone. It's compounded."

Whether you noticed a dramatic uptick in your feelings of disconnection during the last few years or have endured an ongoing struggle, you are not alone. This is how low-grade social anxiety works. This chapter gives you the inside scoop on skills and patterns you can actively shift. If you wish for deeper connections but it feels risky and scary, I don't want you to settle. Here's what you need to demystify this sneaky anxious pattern.

DISCONNECTION HAPPENS ON THE INSIDE

Isolation is often caused by situational factors—a job change and relocation to a new city, a pandemic, a divorce, or a child left on their own for many different reasons. This experience of isolation is usually temporary and resolves when the situation does.

But more pervasive feelings of disconnection and isolation are fueled by a perception that you're missing out, combined with an exhausting battle in your head as to why. It's a feeling of deep longing. There's a gap between what you hope to get from your relationships and what you're experiencing from them. You might feel confused or defeated if your efforts have failed while you watch others seemingly connect easily. *It should be easy*, you tell yourself, but it seems so mysterious and overwhelming. If for whatever reason you didn't learn the skills of connection, attachment, or friendship as a child, your immediate and understandable impulse may be to step back and self-protect.

For some, anxious withdrawal and the isolation it causes are severe enough to meet the criteria for a diagnosis of social anxiety disorder. But for many more, these feelings linger below the surface. If you're in this category, you function fine and manage life with an adequate number of acquaintances and colleagues. But it's a dull ache of *not enough* and wishing for more, like Darcy.

People generally believe that social anxiety is all about people. That's true, sort of. You need people to feel socially anxious, just as you need dogs to be afraid of dogs. Or do you? Remember, anxiety happens on the inside, driven by anticipation of what could go wrong, so the actual people or actual dogs aren't as important as your perception of the dogs or the people. Remember, too, that when we're anxious, we are seeking certainty and working to eliminate all risk, which is particularly difficult to achieve when dealing with people's unpredictability. Humans are inconsistent, at times hard to read, and full of their own patterns and weirdnesses and assumptions. Relationships shift and evolve. They're fluid and risky. Anxiety hates this. When anxiety can't get the certainty it wants, people retreat and avoid. If the goal is to eliminate all risk, how can you step into the murky arena of new relationships or experiences?

Alice experienced this roadblock. She was a single woman in her early thirties who came to see me because of her depressed mood and overall feeling that her life was stuck. The sources of her sadness were clear to her: a boring job, a long-standing hatred of our cold New Hampshire winters, and aching loneliness. She wanted to find a long-term relationship, and while she had "some nice friends" whom she saw now and then, there was no one to whom she felt particularly close. It was notable to me that, even though Alice could list all the aspects of her life that felt unsatisfying, she seemed stumped when it came to changing any of them. "I know what's wrong; I just can't fix it," she told me. She imagined living in a southern climate where she could go to the beach. She wanted a job with more responsibility and challenge, and an environment full of coworkers to whom she could relate. She even fantasized about living in a house with others, sharing costs and eating meals together. Living alone in her apartment was too isolating, she said.

Did Alice have the external resources to make these changes? Yes. She had saved money to relocate to another city, and her professional skills were in high demand. But as we talked, I recognized a pattern common in people who acknowledge their disconnection and yet stay stuck in it. While her expressed plans and hopes were clear—new job, communal housing with roommates she could enjoy, and colleagues she could relate to—she also wanted to have everything in place before she even considered a move. *What if I make all these changes and it doesn't work out?* was the thought that kept her immobile. She was banking on a *sure* thing before she would try even *one* thing. Her need for certainty was so powerful that it kept her from stepping out of her isolated routine.

What if I go on a first date and the person is a loser?

What if I change jobs and after three months my coworkers don't like me?

What if I overhaul my life and I'm still lonely?

Alice chose to stay in her apartment in this cold northern state at a boring job. Sadly, she kept her risk low, but her mood and her sense of connection stayed low too.

As Alice's situation illustrates, inner isolation worsens when this overall need for certainty and elimination of risk (a part of all anxiety struggles) specifically doubles down on avoiding judgment or rejection. She worried that people wouldn't like her. She imagined more painful rejection and chose the option of avoidance, which would seem to hurt less. But this strategy of avoiding all judgment will never work for Alice, and it won't work for you because as social creatures, we are hardwired to judge. Finding connection while avoiding judgment isn't going to happen.

The need to take stock of each other is a key part of our social makeup. Knowing the difference between safety and threat is vital to our very survival. So we judge—all the time. Are you a friend? Are you an enemy? Will you hurt me? Will you help me? Shall we perpetuate the species or shall I look elsewhere? Of course, modern times have allowed us to judge more haphazardly or superficially, or so it seems. Are you funny? Do you have good taste in shoes? How old are your kids? Will you hike up a mountain with me? Would you be a good roommate? A good business partner?

Whether the content of these judgments is lifesaving or seemingly incidental, the quest is still the same: can we connect? And while this type of modern social connection may not be directly critical to your actual physical survival in the twenty-first century, connectedness impacts your emotional belonging and well-being. *It still matters greatly as you're looking for a tribe, a connection.*

Left out in the cold. Starved for affection. Lost in a crowd. These expressions reveal how closely our sense of emotional connection is linked to our basic understanding of safety and survival.

SURROUNDED BY PEOPLE, ALONE WITH YOUR THOUGHTS

Alice was lonely and isolated; her avoidance of risk meant she saw few people. But I meet many people who are literally surrounded by others. I often talk to parents who are overwhelmed by the constant demands of young children and a job and other obligations. People are everywhere, and they still feel isolated. They crave both time to themselves—"I just want to take a bath for twenty minutes without someone banging on the bathroom door screaming for me"—and describe themselves as disconnected and lonely. *How can I feel so isolated*, they wonder, *when I am always around people? Why do I feel disconnected when someone always needs something from me?*

Anxiety and depression are both referred to as internalizing disorders, which means you do the bulk of your depressing or anxious thinking inside yourself, by yourself. You may be surrounded by people and even interacting with them, but your anxious "interactions" are a closed loop of you talking to your worry part about what's wrong with *you*. And without any outside perspective, there's little opportunity to challenge your worry's conclusions.

The result is a tighter and tighter spiral of negativity, resulting in even more isolation. Research has found that lonely people tend to be *more self-focused and less responsive to others*. Think about that: people who crave connection, who report feeling lonely, tend to be more internally focused and pay less attention to others' experiences. This isn't a deliberate decision, of course, but it's a patterned anxious response (repetitive negative thinking [RNT]) that feels intuitive and disguises itself as helpful. The response to the problem (going inside to think, analyze, self-criticize) creates more of the problem you're hoping to solve.

When you are worried about judgment, you also share less of your real self with others. You know how you think and feel and are acutely aware of all your shortcomings, but you keep this to yourself, lest others reject you. The problem continues to compound itself. When you don't share yourself, you get little back. You reinforce the belief that no one else feels or thinks the horrible, stupid, scary, insecure things you feel or think. You become even more protective, closed off, and ashamed.

I see this in my practice all the time. Lauren, for example, contacted me during the pandemic because she had just given birth to her second child and was feeling isolated and overwhelmed. I had treated Lauren several years before as a college student when she was having difficulty being away from home and making friends. Back then, Lauren felt like she was watching her peers from a distance, wondering inside how they managed to become close. She would observe others from the periphery, and then spend hours after any social interaction being highly self-critical. During her therapy when she was in college, we worked on recognizing the patterns of her internal dialogue and shifting her powerful (and isolating) belief that if people knew her—really knew her—they'd reject her. She began to make connections with others as she increased her willingness to share more openly, learning how much she had in common with many peers. She began to step into reasonable social risk and consciously interrupt those harsh internal evaluations she once believed to be helpful.

Now Lauren was back. Unsurprisingly, having a second baby during the pandemic reignited some old patterns. Lauren was isolated from friends and family, leaving her alone with her thoughts. She was unable to feel the connection and validation that sustained her. When she felt overwhelmed, she told herself she shouldn't be. When she was exhausted and had thoughts that maybe having a second child was a mistake, she kept them to herself. When her husband tried to touch her but she felt completely disinterested, she worried that she didn't love him as much and that their marriage was in trouble. She went inside, feeling anxious and guilty. The more disconnected she felt, the more she beat herself up.

In our Zoom sessions, I helped Lauren lean into more openness and vulnerability. Anxiety and depression make us amnesiac to our past successes, so I reminded Lauren of what she had learned about sharing with others. She remembered that after her first baby, she was seeing her friends regularly. As a new mom, she received lots of support and good advice. She remembered how her sister warned her, "You'll panic at first, wondering if your life will ever be the same." Her friend told her that sex with her partner was less appealing when she felt as if there was nothing more to give, and that was normal. She'd laughed with her friends about how they'd pay a million dollars for uninterrupted sleep.

That wasn't happening now. The isolation of the pandemic exacerbated Lauren's pattern of closed-off shame. She should have this mothering thing figured out, right? It wasn't her first baby, after all. She should know better and do better. Lauren was quick to recognize the pattern when I reminded her of both her college experience and what she needed after her first baby. Talk to your friends, I told her. Share your thoughts. Tell your husband what you're thinking because he may be kind of freaking out too. He might be afraid to share his inner struggles because he also sees you struggling.

I shared a story of my own. I told her that I have a picture of my husband and me at the top of a mountain in Montana. It's a favorite photograph of us, taken on one of our yearly pre-parent trips out west. We are full of endorphins and joy, smiling broadly, while in the background storm clouds are heading our way. A few days after our first son was born, on a day that I felt overwhelmed with the powerful emotions of new motherhood and unsure how we were going to adjust, I turned the picture face down. When I looked at the two of us, I thought, *We're never gonna hike up a mountain again*, so I hid it from view. Lauren began to cry. You felt this way, too, she realized. Her tears were of relief and connection and permission. Soon after, when she began to open up to others about her worries and doubts, her friends and sister and husband responded with a chorus of "Same here!" and "I get it! I felt this way too!"

A CULTURE OF COMPARISON

Lauren was struggling with a big life transition, one that she believed should be happy and exciting. Here was this wonderful event, yet she wasn't feeling so wonderful—at least not most of the time—so she kept quiet and felt alone. This is not unusual. The experience of disconnection and isolation is often powerful when, by our culture's external measures, we *should* be on top of the world, when it looks like we are doing well, when it appears to others that we've figured it out because that's what we're showing to others.

Our current achievement culture focuses on lists of accomplishments and markers of material success. We judge ourselves and others based on the external results: material wealth and job title and performance, or where our kids go to college. This emphasis on competitive results has produced a level of anxiety in children, teens, and parents that is, to be a bit catastrophic, epidemic. I've worked with many successful, achievement-focused people, and here's what I see: the more competent they and their get-it-done peers appear on the outside, the harder it can be to share their own struggles. Everyone thinks everyone else is doing great. And the more they believe they're supposed to be happy and excited and grateful *all the time*, the worse it gets. Isolation thrives. Shame festers. Disconnection deepens.

Are you someone who has learned to value yourself (and value others) based on doing, on achievements? Do you often judge yourself based on results, on what you achieve? Me, too! And that's not all bad. It's normal and positive to feel proud and competent when we accomplish things. The trap, however, is believing that everyone else is doing it easier or better than you and that the external results they are showing to the world are the full story. We compare houses, kids, marriages, career trajectories, income, bodies, and we believe that what others are showing us—the visible results or the curated images of their life—is the full reality. Then we compare it to our own untidy journey.

Isn't it funny how we know the mess of *our* story, but we're so quick to believe that someone else's story is neat and smooth? Curiously, we know that others are curating their image (because we do it ourselves) and still fall for the ruse. My mentor and depression expert Dr. Michael Yapko says, "When you compare your inside to someone else's outside, it's not a fair fight."

KNOW IT ALL, BUT DO IT ALONE

Undeniably, technology and social media have made comparison easier and more intense, but the trap is not new. Research compiled in the early 1980s looked at social comparison and its contribution to disconnection and loneliness. The researchers found that people who compared the quality and quantity of their friendships to others often became chronically lonely and disconnected. Even without the help of technology, we have long been riddled with this fear of exposure and the isolation that follows: "I can't truly connect with you because what I show the world is too different than what is really happening in my life. I must keep my distance."

Admittedly, technology turbocharges this situation; social comparisons are now an instantaneous click away with a seemingly endless array of people in your current life and past life, and even never in your life until that moment. Social media simultaneously offers connection while fueling our competitive drive and distorting our view of others. It's a confusing, flip-flopping game we play, picking and choosing what to show others, what to share of our family and professional lives, and what to filter and hide. We have access to what others are doing (connection) while we can experience rejection in real time (isolation).

And there's more. Our internal social struggles are heightened by another enduring set of age-old values: our dominant American culture still loves the storylines of the self-made person and the overnight success. Historically and currently, we admire rugged individualism and the ability to make it on our own. Perhaps you're reading this and dismissing these as old-fashioned tropes. I too associate these "loner" values with images of the Marlboro Man and Dirty Harry. Macho cowboys and tough, silent rogues are as outdated as cigarette ads in this highly connected, modern world, right? Wrong. These values are still advertised as strengths. Progress has been made, but not as much as we'd like to believe. Once again, we see problems of sharing too little, disguised as sharing too much.

Despite a common perception that young people are more open about their struggles, self-reliance is still a powerful message among young adults. Research done in 2020 examining the loneliness and disconnection felt by eighteen- to thirty-four-year-olds during the pandemic found that societal pressure to "cope on your own" remains a relevant value that impacts mental wellness. As lead author Ellie Lisitsa writes, "Culture may also play a role, as research suggests that young adults in the U.S. may seek social support less than other age groups due to developmental pressure for increased autonomy combined with cultural values of individualism and self-reliance."

Even though we don't want to close off parts of ourselves, women in particular are often given the message that to be successful, they need to do just that. "Society may have told some women we could do anything," author and leadership coach Rachel Simmons writes, "but it omitted a huge catch: we can't be who we are while we're doing it."

When we apply this approach of going it alone to our emotional, social, and professional struggles, the cost is high. But from my perspective as a therapist treating anxiety, this coping-on-your-own approach, especially in high-achieving environments, is common. It means scheduling a closed-door consultation with your repetitive negative thoughts; but when you only talk to you, then you are relying on your own beliefs, fears, and catastrophic predictions to determine what to share and what to withhold. With reported rates of loneliness up to 50 percent higher in young adults than the elderly in the United States, we must conclude that another generation has bought into these cultural norms.

Moreover, let us not forget that cultural influence happens in big groups and small, with family often the most powerful cultural generator of all. It's commonly the first place people learn not to talk about or share the most universal of human experiences. The family code of secrecy and the demand to look good are as potent as ever. Social media makes us feel as if we are sharing more, but the forces of comparison, achievement, and isolation are still thriving. Our "sharing" remains bathed in the fear of judgment and failure.

I certainly see improvement in the willingness of parents to talk about their child's struggles with anxiety and depression. Recognition of the pervasiveness of these problems has helped. But I also see many families that cannot and will not acknowledge the patterns of anxiety, depression, alcoholism, and abuse that go back generations. Such patterns are either denied completely or disguised with careful euphemisms, despite the commonality. Last year, I began an interesting experiment. When giving presentations to audiences of parents, educators, or other mental health providers, I have started asking this question: does anyone here have one of those families that is free of anxiety, depression, or substance use? No one—truly not a single person—has ever raised a hand.

CONFLICT AVOIDANCE: KEEPING THE PEACE, KEEPING YOUR DISTANCE

People say to me, "I hate conflict." As do I. It's like a little kid telling me they hate shots, to which I reply, "It'd be kind of weird if you loved them, don't you think?" Conflicts are like shots: when they are important, we step in and deal with the discomfort, but most of us don't seek them out unnecessarily. And like it or not, conflicts, like shots, are routine occurrences of modern human existence. But what if you don't know how or when to step into the discomfort of conflict? What if you are so afraid of conflict that you don't let people know what's going on inside of you? How does that impact your relationships? How does that foster isolation?

If you struggle with feeling disconnected, conflict avoidance is another pattern to investigate. Problems arise when, out of fear or worry or lack of experience, your go-to for dealing with conflict is complete avoidance. Like all avoidance, it works fabulously in the short term. You feel relieved to dodge the pain, the difficult conversation, the emotional awkwardness. As a long-term approach, however, it backfires. You avoid immediate distress, but as we all have experienced, the unresolved issues hang around and fester. A consistent desire to avoid conflict often leads to increased problems over time—capitulation and resentment, to name a few—and then ultimately more avoidance: another downward spiral that keeps you from the depth of connection you truly want.

If you were raised in an anxious family, conflict avoidance may have been modeled for you. If you had an anxious parent, you likely learned that conflict was to be avoided or denied because anxious people—and especially those who struggle with inner isolation—are often very sensitive to real or perceived conflict and rejection. The goal of anxious families is certainty and comfort, and addressing conflict, even in very productive ways, is uncomfortable! Now, as an adult you may continue to avoid conflict because you never saw it being handled well and you have no idea how to address it in a healthy way. What did you learn about navigating conflict? How was rejection handled and supported? Did anyone help you find your way? Was conflict viewed as normal (albeit painful) or as a crisis?

If you come from an abusive or chaotic background, conflict wasn't avoided but was scary and threatening. Your experience tells you, rightly so, that you have reason to fear stepping into that arena. Like the person who comes from a conflict-avoidant family, you don't have the skills or the belief that confrontation improves the situation or allows for satisfying connection. Conflict is dangerous. When children experience uncontrolled and traumatic conflict, a few things may happen as they get older: they may model the violence or chaos they were taught, they may seek to avoid all conflict, or they may move between feeling and behaving out of control and then feeling ashamed, scared, and shut down.

No matter the source of your avoidance, these learned patterns and beliefs meant lost opportunities to practice handling conflict in a healthy way as you matured. If you never saw the benefits or even the possibility of a positive outcome, not only do you stay disconnected from others, but you may close yourself off from your own unexpressed thoughts, emotions, and opinions. Such was the case with Colton.

When I met Colton, he was in his late thirties with a solid career as an electrician and three young children. He knew he felt anxious in an omnipresent, simmering way, and he had good reason to be. His childhood was one of violence. He witnessed his parents fighting almost daily, and their addictions led to repeated arrests and absences. All Colton wanted, he told me, was to fit in: to have a calm and predictable life, a family to love, a group of friends that he could hang out with, and to be involved in his children's lives.

On the surface he had done extremely well meeting these goals. Based on his history, Colton was remarkable for his conscious striving for stability and kindness. Unlike his siblings, he chose not to drink at all. By the time he was in his mid-twenties, he owned his own home. He was the guy who always helped his buddies move. He met Beth in college, and they married soon after graduation. He referred to her as his best friend.

So what was the problem? Beth convinced Colton to come to therapy because she felt distant from him and didn't know what else to do. "She says I'm so nice that it drives her nuts," he told me. "I do everything I can for our family, but she says it feels like I'm a million miles away. She thinks I'm depressed."

Colton denied feeling depressed. He felt successful professionally and loved participating in activities with his family. He thrived on keeping busy with house projects and coaching his daughter's soccer team. But it didn't take long for me to understand that internally Colton was on constant alert, making sure he did everything to stay ahead of conflict. His accommodating style meant he rarely expressed an opinion—or any negative emotion. What did he want for dinner? Anything is great, he'd respond. Where should they go on vacation? You choose, he told Beth. When a friend cancelled on an event at the last minute, Colton brushed it off, even though this friend had repeatedly let him down in this way.

Colton's anxiety didn't keep him from doing things, so no one saw him as anxious. But he was. The fear of conflict was so powerful and catastrophic inside him that he didn't allow himself to feel anything negative—and to not feel anything negative about his wife or kids or boss or friends, he needed to stay disconnected. "His kindness doesn't even feel real anymore," Beth said. "I feel guilty for feeling anything negative toward him because he never shows me anything negative about anything!"

Colton's story may sound extreme, but the process is familiar. Colton was inside with his worry, believing his own story about conflict and safety. And who can blame him? This is one of the ways that anxiety connects with trauma. The strategies he learned both protected him as a child and absolutely helped him have positive relationships as an adult—to a point. He needed to keep a pleasant distance as dictated by his worry. The honest and open connection that Beth sought was confusing and scary to him. He did not know what to do.

His therapy focused on how to connect with Beth and his own feelings in a way that wasn't dictated by his past experiences of conflict and violence. Colton believed he had two approaches to choose from: disconnected and safe, or out of control and scary. He needed to learn that conflict did not have to mean violence, and there were plenty of relationships in Colton's life where being helpful, agreeable, and self-protective worked fine. Those skills had great value, just not all the time and definitely not all the time in his marriage.

Colton slowly learned to express opinions, disagree, and even say no to friends' requests for help. He needed to set boundaries and tolerate the discomfort he felt when others were angry or disappointed, including Beth. He was allowed to say no to people as he ran his business. His children were young when we started working together, but they are going to turn into teenagers one day. They'll get angry and even rebellious, and he'll need to handle that. Relationships and parenting are dynamic, so he continues to learn and model these skills every day: tolerating uncertainty and updating his RNTs, trusting that he is different from his own parents, and working to interrupt the patterns of his family legacy by sharing his emotions and thoughts in healthy ways.

People don't often recognize how anxiety leads to isolation and disconnection, but I'm hoping you now have better insight into how our common patterns of anxiety can sneak into relationships, keeping us from authentically connecting with others. The patterns in this book overlap, so as you think about the prospect of dealing with conflict, you might overestimate the risk and catastrophize the outcome of *any conflict*, as was the case with Colton. Recognize that you may have a lack of experience with healthier outcomes and a great ability to imagine terrible ones. Your imagination teams up with anxiety's need for certainty, and the result is avoidance of many things: judgment, awkwardness, rejection, conflict, and the unpredictable course of learning through trial and error.

Of course, it's not all or nothing. We want flexibility and adaptability, depending on the situation. You needn't share everything with anyone, nor strive to connect with everyone. In addition to positive connection, you are also developing self-reliance and autonomy in certain areas of your life. This balance of skills is the opposite of the global avoidance and withdrawal that anxiety demands.

Give yourself a dose of compassion as you learn about your patterns and work on adjusting them.

WHAT TO DO

Question Your Own (Rigid) Perspective About You

Those people who feel most isolated are often surprised to discover, once we start looking at their patterns, how rigidly and sometimes fiercely connected they are to their own perceptions. It's an interesting revelation because if they are more introverted or quiet or conflict-avoidant, they've always been viewed as compliant or passive. When asked to make a decision or express an opinion, they defer. They don't speak up in class or in meetings. That external compliance, however, often belies unshakable internal opinions and conclusions, usually about themselves.

Owning this rigidity and then questioning those rigid conclusions represent a vital first step.

I remember working with a quiet and sensitive woman who was struggling to make friends. Early in our conversations, I listened as she conveyed some strong opinions about herself and friendships, opinions that were clearly working against her:

She wasn't talkative enough to have friends.

People were turned off by her voice.

> She worked hard to make sure she never offended anyone, and yet still didn't have friends, so kindness didn't work.
>
> Most people make their close friends early in life, so she'd missed her chance.

I also noticed that she reflexively rejected any compliment I gave her, however small, and dismissed any questioning of her conclusions. She was gently combative.

"You see yourself as kind and agreeable, and that's true externally. You are certainly a kind person," I told her. "But you're very rigid and opinionated internally about who you are and how others see you. You are, in this area of your life, a stubborn but ill-informed expert."

This statement stunned her. How was she stubborn? And ill-informed? Those were the qualities of a loud, know-it-all blowhard! She was the opposite of someone like that! She was full of doubt and insecurities.

On the outside, she was not at all stubborn or bossy. When dealing with the world, she was often timid and accommodating. But her powerful internal conclusions went unchallenged. She committed fully to her own perceptions. I'll tell you what I told her: if you continue to bat away compliments as fake or inaccurate *(That person doesn't really mean that)*, if you hold fast to the mantras that support your disconnection *(No one feels the way I do, I'm different from other people)*, if you refuse to allow others' opinions about you to count at all, then you will miss out on the gift of sometimes being wonderfully, delightfully *wrong*.

How do you remain locked into perceptions about you that need updating? Are you committed to long-held beliefs about you that might be inaccurate? Are you capable of accepting others' perceptions about you? How do you receive compliments from others? Do you quickly dismiss or qualify the praise? You can begin to shift this pattern by accepting compliments with a simple thank-you. Notice what it feels like to just *let it sink in.* If you want to connect with others, then their thoughts and opinions and likes and dislikes must also matter. If not, you remain a lonely and isolated party of one, playing the same worn-out tunes.

Be a Curious Student: Observe and Learn

Social skills are learned. If you did not have good role models as a child, it's not too late to start observing and picking up tips. This requires an external focus, the opposite of what your worrying demands. Pay attention. Be a curious student. Notice how some people overshare or others withhold. Have you ever had a conversation with someone who answers yes-or-no questions with only a "yes" or "no"? Makes it hard to keep a conversation going, doesn't it? How about talking to a person who dominates the conversation but never inquires about others? How do you connect with that person? Who in your life is good at connecting? How do they do it?

Knowing what and when to share is a skill that develops with practice and experience. Give yourself permission to observe and learn, and then step in. When you start off in the role of the observer, you can relieve some of the pressure. Sit in the audience where less is required of you. Observe with curiosity and imitate what others do. Imagine that you are listening to a concert, admiring the skill of the violinists, and it's so compelling you even contemplate taking some violin lessons. Or compare it to watching an instructional video on YouTube about dog grooming or cooking enchiladas or choosing the right eyeglass frames for your face. Be open to learning something new and see what loosens up inside when you take this stance. Can you enjoy learning? Have you done so in the past? Consciously notice when the habitual and self-critical voice arrives. *There it is*, you can say to yourself. *There's that automatic response that gets me to retreat. This is what I'm working to shift.*

And one last reminder: Connection requires a dose of discomfort and courage, but you don't have to push yourself all the time, particularly if you've not been shown *how*. Allow yourself to be a hesitant beginner. No one expects you to hear the symphony once (or even twenty times), then pick up a violin and play perfectly. That all-or-nothing approach is what kept Alice stuck. She wouldn't mess around with any changes until she was certain of the outcome. Learning doesn't work that way.

Risk Authentic and Deep Connection—Toes in the Water

So you've observed and learned and bumped up your social skills. You've pushed yourself to take a few risks. Or maybe you already have lots of connections, and you competently manage the social requirements of life and work and family. Your social skills are solid and your relationships feel *okay*, but you hope to deepen some of these connections with your friends or partner or family.

If you recognize this level of connection exists but don't have it, it often becomes what you crave. It's the stuff of friendship fantasy we often see portrayed in novels and movies. (I think of the New Year's Eve scene from *Sex in the City* where Carrie travels across the snowy city in ridiculous shoes to Miranda's apartment, knowing from a short phone call that Miranda is desperately alone and lonely.) You seek the relationships where you can share who you truly are. You want to be able to feel vulnerable and validated while talking honestly about what's going on inside of your messy life or doubt-filled head. You recognize it when you see it from afar and sense it's what you want, but how to create it is a mystery. It's what socially anxious kids are describing to me when they share their dreams of a *best friend.* And it's a process that requires practice, patience, and risk.

More than twenty years ago, I moved to the small city where I still live. My husband was traveling for his job, we had a baby, and I didn't know a single person. I wanted—needed!—friends, so I immediately joined a gym where I met many great women, including one of my to-this-day closest friends. She became part of a very small group that sees my true self, the many parts of me.

When we were just getting to know each other, I was both careful and hopeful. I was feeling unsure if she wanted to be my friend, because personality-wise she was more reserved than I was. I was louder and messier. She was beautiful and organized and so kind and remains so today. (Side note: she continues to be a role model for me on how to gracefully keep one's mouth shut when one should.) One day I called to ask a random question and I still remember the sentence she said that convinced me we could be friends: "Oh, dear God, if I have to sit here and play trucks on the carpet for one more minute, I think I'm going to lose my mind." *Oh, thank you, thank you,* I thought. I can be real with this person. Parenting toddlers is boring and monotonous sometimes. Guard down, small risk taken, truth shared. This was the start of our deep friendship, toes in the water.

As you move in the direction of authentic connection, these are key points to remember.

- *Sharing and connecting have a big sweet spot, not a tiny bull's-eye.* Moving out of a pattern of inner isolation is not an exact science, but anxious people often get trapped in the myth of exactitude. Like most aspects of being a human, it's trial and error with wiggle room and adjustments, a process of hits and misses that lasts a lifetime. You *practice*, like with pickleball or cooking or being a therapist. I have a private *practice*! As long as I continue to do this job, I will not arrive at some professional finish line where I know all I need to know. I am constantly adjusting and learning. Relationships work the same way.

- *Be patient.* When you wish to deepen connection and decrease your inner isolation, you must take some risk by sharing part of you, but it doesn't happen all at once. Pace yourself. Don't spill all your secrets when the relationship or friendship is brand-new—and if others overwhelm you with too much information too quickly, you can take a step back and pay attention to your boundaries. I had many false starts when looking to make new friends. A woman I briefly became friendly with talked money immediately and frequently, telling me how much her husband made and what they paid for their house or their cars. Not my thing! It felt weird. We're not friends.
- *Find your tribe.* Join groups with shared interests: walking, chorus, church committees, Little League baseball/softball, bird watching, cooking, and so on. You will feel awkward. You will try to convince yourself not to go. Go anyway.
- *Therapy can help if you struggle to share your "true" self or have shame about your story or experiences.* With a compassionate therapist, you're able to talk about your inner self, let those unspoken secrets see the light of day. Another human being will hear them and accept them, and you'll both be okay. Many times, a therapy client tells me something they've

never shared, never spoken about to anyone. And it's good. Even if the story or the thoughts or feelings are traumatic and horrible, they are no longer unspeakable. I've heard similar stories to theirs, and I let them know that. When we speak the unspeakable, when we share the unshared, the power of the secrecy cannot hold. Therapy may be where you start working on the goal of taking that *practice* out into your world.

- *Not everyone deserves your authentic self.* You get to choose who has access to that part of you. I tell my young clients that when they have something important to share, treat that information like a little bird that they're holding gently in their cupped hands. Offer that information to those who will care for the little bird and treat your disclosure with the respect and kindness it deserves.
- *Recognize how exhausting and tricky professional connections can be.* If you're striving to achieve in your career, the messages about how to succeed are soaked in warnings about being strategic and cautious about what you reveal, but this can take a toll. As Rachel Simmons describes, it's exhausting to work so hard at holding back: "The cost is huge. When you don't have access to your authentic self, you lose a natural engine of creativity and connection. You're less invested in your work. And you're exhausted." The corollary lesson learned here is that if you have choices, pick the job or company that best fits the unreserved you.

Cultivate Different Levels of Connection

I described my close friend earlier as one of a small group who sees the most vulnerable parts of me. *A small group*. Additionally, I have many friends who make up a whole cornucopia of connection, an abundant supply of humans who meet all sorts of different needs. My gym buddies know my competitive side and my swearing skill, not something I generally haul out in a professional context. (I'm not global!) My college roommate met me and my husband when we were all so young, so she knows my marriage through that unique lens. I have professional pals who run the gamut of connection, from my friend and writing partner to a few valued mentors to once-a-year companions at conferences whom I love to meet for dinner. My family members know most of me, but some know more than others.

People often have ideas or myths about connection that make it harder to get what they want. They may believe that more superficial or occasional levels of connection don't count. Or that connection is always earnest and meaningful. Know that there are varied types, different levels, and different "eras" of connection with the same person, within the same relationship.

We also can treat connection too seriously, raising pressures and expectations for every interaction to be meaningful. As mentioned earlier, play is a wonderful way to connect. Physical movement, games, and laughter are the opposite of anxiety's preferred state of high alert and hypervigilance. Allowing yourself to connect with joy and silliness, rather than seriousness and pressure and criticism, is the opposite of what anxiety wants. After these last few years of threat, fear, and loss, opening yourself up to playful connection is needed!

In 2021, Kristin Tippett of the *On Being* podcast interviewed Esther Perel, who spoke about how people "come back to life" after trauma, "how people connect to this quality of aliveness, of vibrancy, of vitality, of renewal" after adversity:

> And we began discussing that there's something about when you can once again take risks, because it means that you are not completely trapped in a state of vigilance, when you can once again play or experience pleasure or joy, because it means you are not completely wrapped in the sense of dread. You can't be on guard and let go. And playfulness comes with a certain element of letting go.

Actively Offer Support to Others

Because anxiety and depression are both internally focused states, researchers and clinicians have long held that actively helping others positively impacts mental and physical health. Decades of data show that volunteering improves mood, decreases self-focus and rumination, and increases problem-solving skills. Logistically speaking, it increases opportunities to connect with others in the community. When I was new to town, I joined a local volunteer organization that supports women and children in crisis. This is where I connected with many other women. During the first rollout of the Covid vaccines, I knew many retired healthcare professionals who volunteered to administer the injections, and they were immensely appreciated.

A wonderful example of such active connection is pairing young children with "grandfriends." Such programs have been around for decades but are growing in popularity due to the measured benefits to both groups and because of the 2015 Evan Briggs documentary *The Growing Season*, which highlighted the amazing benefits of the intergenerational program at Providence Mount St. Vincent in Seattle, Washington. In 1991, a childcare center and preschool were established on the premises of a senior living facility. Briggs was interested in how our modern society deals with the elderly, so she spent a year filming there, documenting how the young children and elderly residents interacted. She discovered more than she expected. In her 2015 Tedx Talk, Briggs said this: "I think what I grew to understand in working on this project is that the act of just being present with somebody is a way to acknowledge their inherent value as a human."

Helping other people bolsters your own self-concept; you see yourself as a person who contributes and matters. Many schools have embraced the benefit of volunteerism for teens and now include community service hours for graduation. A group of researchers led by Parissa Ballard at Wake Forest University went even further with their recommendations for connection, seeing it not as ancillary but therapeutically essential. In an article published in May 2021, they strongly advocated for the incorporation of volunteer work as a part of *treatment* for depressed teens, writing that "we propose that including volunteering as a component of clinical treatment approaches for teen depression can be a powerful intervention for adolescents."

During the pandemic lockdown, and then as schools were beginning to reopen in the fall of 2020 (and then again in 2021), I told everyone who would listen to implement what I simply termed "Brighten Someone Else's Day, Day." I wanted schools, families, and organizations to pick a day of the week (or two—or seven for that matter!) and instruct everyone to do three simple acts to brighten someone else's day. "You don't even have to know the person," I said. "The acts can be small. But it needs to be consistent, verbalized, and embraced as a value." This being-kinder thing is not an original concept, but I wanted it assigned and endorsed because Covid made our connection muscles rusty. Many children lost a year or two of engaging socially.

When we're out of practice or missing the skill altogether, making it conscious and effortful helps it become more automatic. I recommend you try it with your family.

What can you do deliberately to offer support? How can you increase your odds of connecting with others in this context of giving of yourself? How can you shift out of that internal focus?

And how will you talk yourself out of making the effort? Are you not smart enough, caring enough, organized enough? Too busy? What old voices will suck you in? How will you convince yourself that it won't help? Will you think too much? Will you go all or nothing, and choose to opt for nothing? Is this how you stay isolated?

Actively Seek Help Too

In addition to offering help to others, seeking social support also increases well-being and decreases loneliness because reaching out for help is an active process. I know it feels risky to ask, but *not asking* is even riskier to your well-being and relationships. Passivity is where anxiety and depression go to breed. I often talk to people who want help but expect or hope that others will know what they need. This would make things easier, wouldn't it, if others could know what you needed and then offered it, minus the vulnerability of asking? Do you fall into the trap of believing that someone who really loved you would know what you need without you having to ask? Let's get rid of that one for good, shall we? That idea—"If you really loved me, you'd *know*"—is nonsense. Increase the odds of getting what you need by communicating directly. (Again, if you have no idea how to do this, therapy can help teach you those skills. If no one taught you, you're not supposed to know; it's learned.) Inner isolation is strengthened by *not asking, not seeking, not articulating.* Being passive and avoidant will *not get you what you want.*

Speaking of passivity, pay attention to how you are using social media. As I discussed earlier, social media use can quickly deteriorate into negative comparison. Interestingly, higher social media use during the pandemic was associated with higher levels of loneliness, but this was offset a bit if the social media was used for social support seeking. Ellie Lisitsa and colleagues found a complicated relationship between social media and social support seeking that seems to hinge on this aspect of passivity versus activity, but they conclude in general that social media isn't helpful: "There is a piece of social media use that has an adaptive support seeking function, but overall social media use is associated with increased loneliness during the pandemic." Now that we are out of the crisis of the pandemic, how will the impacts continue to affect us moving forward?

QUESTIONS FOR PONDERING AND JOURNALING
What were the messages you received about sharing and connecting? Was there a spoken or unspoken prohibition about airing dirty laundry or family secrets?
Who was, is, or can be a role model for you for healthy connection? (Hint: It needs to be a real person and someone you actually know.)
What skill or quality do you have that helps you connect, and what do you need to develop or amend?
How have you shared your skills or talents or self in the past? What was the result? How could you do that again?

CHAPTER FIVE

CREATING CHAOS AND THE LURE OF BUSYNESS

Sneaky Pattern: How Being Busy and Overscheduled Both Add to and Masquerade Our Anxiety and Stress

There is more to life than increasing its speed.

—Mohandas Gandhi

It's not enough to be busy, so are the ants. The question is, what are we busy about?

—Henry David Thoreau

Hard work pays off. This has been an accepted human value for a very long time. The Roman poet Horace, who died in 8 BC, proclaimed, "Life grants nothing to us mortals without hard work."

But newer to our culture is the obsession, the adoration, the worshipping even, of "busy." It's not about what many *must do* to survive and provide, but an admiration for how much we're doing at once and how stressed we are while doing it. Being overbooked and overstressed has become a social badge of honor, and let me say that working hard to provide for a family is clearly not what I'm talking about here. This busyness is not a pattern driven by survival or necessity, but a social and anxious pattern with very different demands. It is not about working two or three jobs to pay rent or finishing a shift to then go care for an aging parent. Busyness is a privilege, based on choice and not force. It is the result, in part, of the very modern, and privileged, pursuit of the elusive and coveted work/life balance.

The problem, as I see it, is the unhelpful definition of *balance* in this context. It seems off to me, distorted in a single direction. In the culture of busyness, there's no balance by subtraction, no balance achieved by doing *less*. It's balance through addition, trying to balance the teeter-totter of our lives by adding more and more to both sides of the seesaw. Can you see the image of the board straining and bending? "Work hard, play hard" is the slogan. We just need a way to do it better with the same amount of time (or by "creating" time by sleeping less), to bend but not break under the weight of it all.

Is it working? Not really. Women in particular are feeling the demands of their obligations. They have endeavored to make family and work life more equal and balanced, pushing back against a gender-defined division of labor in families. But women's desire to find balance and fairness has not meshed with our ability to pull it off. The statistics—before and after the pandemic—consistently find that women do significantly more housework and childcare, regardless of income and employment status. In a May 2020 article in the *New York Times*, during the height of the lockdown, Claire Cain Miller reported, "Seventy percent of women say they're fully or mostly responsible for housework during lockdown, and 66 percent say so for childcare—roughly the same shares as in typical times." What is the result? Research consistently finds that women are twice as likely to be diagnosed with an anxiety disorder compared to men.

We say we want to change these dynamics—and we mean it—but are still unable to do what needs to be done. As we dive into this pattern of busyness and what I describe as the culture of created chaos, let's look at the forces at play. How did we get here? And how do we stay here? Does a pattern of busyness make us more anxious?

Do you live in a chronically stressed state of busyness? Do you routinely describe your life in these terms?

Do you often feel like there is too much to do, so that you're unable to do anything with your full attention or presence?

How do you internally keep the chaos going? What most influences your busyness?

What do you believe—and like—about being busy?

THE LURE OF MORE, THE MYTH OF MULTITASKING

In 1992 my husband and I took our new marriage and irritated cat to Pennsylvania, where my husband had landed a job with a manufacturing company. Each year the company hosted an end-of-the-year holiday dinner where employees were recognized for a variety of accomplishments. Almost thirty years later, I still remember one dinner vividly. We sat in a hotel banquet room at a large, round table with several other couples as various bosses announced retirements and handed out length-of-service awards. Then the company's president came to the podium to offer one senior executive special recognition. During the past several months, the president told us, Hugh's child with special needs had undergone open-heart surgery and dealt with other medical complications. And yet, despite this very challenging and stressful time, Hugh had closed a major deal. His dedication to the company went above and beyond. He was able to balance work and family. I was incredulous. *Really?* I thought. I scanned the faces around our table. *Really??*

I already knew that being the first to arrive in the morning and the last to leave at night was admired and rewarded. BlackBerries and car phones were exciting new corporate gadgets to get more done, to stay constantly connected. As Hugh walked to the podium to receive some token of appreciation, the message was clear: his ability to *handle it all* was the standard to achieve. I quickly glanced over at Hugh's wife, trying to guess what she was thinking, and I repeatedly poked my husband's leg under the table. He did not need to guess what I was thinking.

Please. There was no balance. If Hugh's job performance didn't suffer—and clearly it didn't—then something else did. But in 1992, this idea that we could do it all and have it all was gaining momentum, and technology was there to help.

In the late 1990s and early 2000s, multitasking became the hot new skill touted as *the* way to gain the competitive advantage. Multitasking was listed on résumés. Courses were taught at business schools. The new handheld electronic devices were advertised as multitasking enhancers that would help us *get more done*. The enthusiasm was, however, short-lived, particularly among those who study how brains actually work.

By 2008, study after study showed both the inefficiencies and risks of multitasking. One study found that multitasking was akin to smoking marijuana or experiencing a drop in IQ of several points. Gloria Mark, a researcher at the University of California–Irvine, studied interruptions among office workers and found that it took an average of twenty-three minutes to recover from an email or phone call interruption and fully reengage in the original task. She also found that many who were interrupted then worked faster to complete the task but paid a price. Interrupted workers who were then required to task-switch experienced more stress, higher frustration, and increased time pressure. The impact of multitasking while driving (texting and even talking on a cellphone) has been well-documented, with impairment similar to driving drunk.

People who multitask want to believe (or hope) they can do it all, but it's just not true. For over fifteen years, neuroscientists have been researching the brain's ability to multitask. The answer to those original questions—Is it possible? Is it beneficial?—is still no. Our brains can't focus fully on more than one task, so attempts to do so mean that something (or someone) is coming up short. Christine Rosen wrote in her 2008 article "The Myth of Multitasking," "When we talk about multitasking, we are really talking about attention: the art of paying attention, the ability to shift our attention, and, more broadly, to exercise judgment about what objects are worthy of our attention." You and I have tried to listen to a partner or child while also trying to read an email. We can't. We choose one because our brains must.

If you continue to believe that you can focus on many things at once, if you set up your life such that you constantly switch from one task to another to meet the day's demands, you are adding to your stress. Researchers sounded the alarm early because they quickly saw the cost of divided attention. The increased expectations for speed, output, and performance through multitasking were unworkable. The science predicted with prescient accuracy where we are now: higher levels of stress, anxiety, attention issues (in children particularly), and depression.

BUSYNESS IS THE NEW IN-GROUND SWIMMING POOL

Are you just *so busy*? It's crazy, right? Your schedule is nuts! And your kids are *so busy*!

Being busy, overscheduled, and stressed is the norm. It has also become the way we show our worth. You'd find it odd if you ran into an acquaintance and they told you how much free time they had, or how they've been coasting through their days without obligation or stress. You'd judge. What are they doing? What does that say about them? Are they lazy? Packed work schedules and too many commitments show us and the world how hard we work and thus how important we are. Our time is *precious* because we have so little of it to share. Busy equals important.

Believe me, busyness is compelling. I know the busy trap well. A few years ago, I was completely overscheduled and exhausted. If I could fit in one more event or one more client, it meant more income. I was putting two sons through college, so it made good sense. That's why I was overscheduled, right? Not so fast. When sociologists look at this trend of busyness, what they find is fascinating. According to current research on busyness, the creation of such a "lifestyle" is not really about money. Busyness, according to a group of researchers led by Columbia Business School professor of marketing Silvia Bellezza, is about increasing social standing and value in the eyes of others. When something is scarce, it becomes a valuable commodity. It's not acceptable to brag openly about money, but if you're busy and your time is coveted, go ahead and boast, boast, boast! You are valuable. Even advertisers work to appeal to our busyness. We need their products, they tell us, because we amazing do-it-all consumers have no time to do it ourselves. Look at us go!

The ad copy for a Keurig coffee maker reads, "We love that this coffee maker makes single servings—perfect for your busy, career-oriented friend who just needs a cup of joe for the road!" Or, even better, an ad for an alarm clock made by Hatch: "This alarm clock gently wakes you up, and it's also a sound machine that can help you fall asleep. Ideal for someone with a packed schedule who suffers from insomnia!"

Bellezza and her colleagues found that "busy" Facebook posts result in perceptions of higher status. A leisurely life, once a sign of privilege, is now looked down upon. The researchers write, "People use social media to publicly display how much they work and complain about leisure time in an attempt to exhibit high status." Being busy and overwhelmed, they observe, is the new humblebrag.

> "Another crazy weekend! And just back from a crazy business trip! (Again!) Had to juggle two soccer games, a wrestling meet, and getting Carla to her babysitting job. I love that the kids are so passionate but hello #exhausted!"

> "When will it end . . . ? My senior is working so hard on college applications, musical theater prescreens, college auditions, schoolwork, VLACS, SAT prep, her job, all during a pandemic! So, so proud of what she can do!"

"Happy Holidays to all of you wonderful friends who I haven't seen in forever. . . . I miss you! Too much work, too little time. If only I could get a box of time under the Christmas tree, instead of a box of wine! LOL!"

And here's the kicker: those who complain the most about work might not be working that much harder. John Robinson studies how Americans use and account for their time. He found that people regularly overestimate the time they work and often underestimate the time they sleep. (Remember that underestimating sleep is also a common attribute of insomniacs.) Interestingly, the higher the *reported* number of hours worked, the more people were off in their estimates. People who estimated they worked seventy-five hours per week were off by an average of thirty hours!

Of course, this modern (privileged) value is being passed down from parents to children. Families tell me how busy they are on a very regular basis. Parents cancel appointments (to see an anxiety specialist) because they can't make their schedules work. Or sometimes they're in my office bemoaning how they had no time to do the therapy homework I assigned or trying to convince me that their overly anxious eleven-year-old is in charge of her twenty-hour-a-week dance schedule. "We don't push her at all," they say. "It's all her." And perhaps that's true. The culture of being busy-on-the-verge-of-chaos is so prevalent that kids no longer need an obsessively driven parent to push them. Their peers, schools, and social media worlds have adopted it as both necessary and admirable; the model is displayed and adulated right before their developing brains.

Rushing from one scheduled activity to another shows our kids that busyness is a way of life. We ascribe little merit to free, unstructured play, and our kids have picked up that value. A teen client of mine described what happens when her father discovers her doing his version of nothing. "He'll say to me, 'If I see you with too much free time, I wonder if you'll regret later that *you didn't do enough now*.' I feel really guilty if I'm not working on something." As a result, she works extremely hard. Free time for her has become something she needs to steal and hide, as if she's sneaking a cookie before dinner. She craves it but can't truly enjoy it. Empty calories.

A few months ago, I agreed to speak to a high school student for a school project, something I'm generally happy to do now and then. I say yes when kids ask. I offered a few options during the week and also told her I was very flexible over the weekend. We needed about fifteen minutes on the phone. She emailed back that she was "just really busy this weekend, so could we find another time?" When I mentioned this to a teacher friend of mine, she said, "Yes, they fetishize their busyness."

If you are in a parenting role, how do your children hear and respond to these messages of busyness and worth?

How do social forces in your family shape your and your children's beliefs about being busy and stressed?

What mixed messages are you sending about the value of busyness and stress?

BUSYNESS AND OVERRESPONSIBILITY: THE CURSE OF THE PEOPLE PLEASER

When the world shut down in March 2020, Nia felt almost euphoric. Back when we all believed it would last a few weeks, maybe a month, she ticked through the many responsibilities that she'd be forced to let go. She had no choice but to say no. It felt like paradise. With a strange combination of shame and relief, she realized that she needed a pandemic to get a break from her pattern of busyness.

Nia knew she overbooked her life. She joked at her inability to say no. She told people it made her feel good to help others and it was her choice to do as much as she did. But inside, it didn't feel like much of a choice. Nia often felt guilty and anxious, burdened by the fear that any refusal to help, however justified, would make her responsible for someone else's suffering.

By doing everything, she hoped to avoid disappointing, angering, or hurting anyone. Of course, it didn't work. Nia was consistently late, frustrating those she left waiting. She often double-booked herself, then had to cancel an obligation at the last minute or try to do both in a rushed, haphazard way.

To experience Nia was to be witness to a stressful and often inauthentic daily life. What was she really feeling? What did she truly want to do? Or not do? She lied often as she worked to meet her obligations. "It was no trouble at all," she'd say, or "I'm so sorry. . . . The traffic made me late!" She smiled almost constantly when out in the world, waving off people's thanks and concerns as they watched her rush from place to place. She stuffed down her simmering resentment whenever it bubbled to the surface. People offered her advice about scheduling or better time management, but that wasn't the issue.

Nia had few genuine connections with others. She was kind and likable, but people often felt annoyed and frustrated with her inability to keep her promises or to be at all genuine about her own feelings or desires. Nia was a people-pleaser who created busyness—and inadvertent chaos—to avoid any overt conflict in her relationships. Over time, however, even those who knew her best came to experience her constant swirling as a bit self-involved and exhausting.

Helping people is a wonderful thing. I help people for a living. I know it feels good, and I'm grateful to all the other helpers out there.

But people-pleasers like Nia who start with a true desire to help may also be fueled by a *need to please*; they burn themselves out seeking approval and avoiding discomfort. It's enticing until it becomes your identity. Like Nia, you end up feeling trapped and disconnected. This type of busyness, this justification for creating chaos, can also be driven by a distorted sense of responsibility, which most certainly contributed to Nia's pattern. She feared being the source of anyone's pain or distress, whether it was somewhat minor (*What if I don't sew all the costumes perfectly for my daughter's play and they look terrible?*) or big and overwhelming (*What if I don't have lunch with my cousin enough and she ends up getting depressed again?*).

Overresponsibility, in its extreme form, can be a type of obsessive-compulsive disorder (OCD). You feel compelled to help because, if you don't, *something terrible will happen*. Saying no and setting boundaries is not an option because you will then have to live with the fear that you were responsible for a terrible outcome. If you can't or don't help for whatever reason, you're dogged by regret and thoughts of responsibility. *What if that person sitting on that bench alone was lost? Why didn't I stop the car and ask if they were okay? That person at work was crying. What if they went home and killed themselves because I minded my own business?* As with other OCD content (remember perfectionism?), this type of tortuous overresponsibility can be misinterpreted by a society that sees it as positive. But while the world admires you from afar, those closest to you, including you, feel the constant anxiety and pressure of not doing enough.

Nia did not have OCD, but her inability to set boundaries, tolerate the disappointment of others, or recognize the cost of her constant busyness took a huge toll. The immediate need to get everything done for everyone and show the world her competence, as with the other examples of busyness described earlier, backfired. Singer Ed Sheeran said it well: "I can't tell you the key to success, but the key to failure is trying to please everyone." Will Nia give up this pattern? I'm not sure, because being less busy, creating less chaos, and letting go of this outsized responsibility for others means making the most frightening move of all: stepping into her own life, with all its feelings and relationships and discomforts. Busyness fosters avoidance, and we know how anxiety loves that.

BUSYNESS AS AVOIDANCE

Busyness is a distraction machine. Living on the brink of mayhem prevents you from being authentically connected to your thoughts, wants, or emotions. As I said in chapter 1, many who treat anxiety (or are managing it on their own) prescribe and embrace distraction as way to handle it, or even worse, to eliminate it. I'm strongly opposed to this approach because it gives the message that you cannot handle what you feel or think, that you will be overpowered by what's inside you. Instead, you create controlled chaos. You seek out an external feeling of socially accepted "overwhelm" that protects you from those moments of stillness. "Stillness?" you groan. Yes, I hear you. I feel you. Hang with me here.

The poet Rumi (1207–1273) wrote, "The quieter you become, the more you are able to hear." And that scares the stuffing out of many of us. So we keep moving, bemoaning our endless to-do lists, wondering out loud how we'll ever get it all done, while adding more to the list. When your life is full of tasks and lists and obligations, you avoid addressing what you need or want to change. You put off decisions until "the time is right," when your life calms down.

But when will that happen? In our frenetic modern world, the ideas of stillness and being alone with one's thoughts have become daunting tasks. If you're around my age, you remember how meditation and mindfulness exploded into the American mainstream in the mid-1990s, mainly through the work of Jon Kabat-Zinn. Even though silent contemplation has been part of many spiritual practices for centuries, it was not something that was normalized or even familiar to most of us when we were young. Unlike many children now, we weren't trained that way. It was another new skill, with a new language, classes, and workshops. Our heads were spinning as we moved from multitasking to mindfulness and then right into smartphones—and practicing mindfulness with our smartphones. We're still spinning.

For all the reasons I've described already, slowing down feels hard for many of us, like learning as an adult to swim or ride a bike. *I have to be still? I have to sit in this mess? I have to learn about myself?* I believe this perception is why many people avoid going to therapy. It sounds *possible* when Oprah says it, but you have stuff to get done and it's tangled inside there. "I don't want to be quiet with my thoughts. I don't want to be alone in my brain. I don't want to question what to do with my life. I don't want to know!"

And sometimes you just don't want to feel. I've heard this sentiment from scores of people: "If I slow down and let myself go there, I'm afraid I'll never get out. If I start to cry [or get angry, or feel scared, or . . . , I'll never be able to stop. Just better to keep busy." Better to keep moving.

The truth, however, is that cultivating a life of busyness does not get rid of anything. Anger, resentments, worry, and grief are human emotions which will both find their way out—*force* their way out—and drag you back inside to wrestle with them. You can attempt to get rid of the inside discomfort and the outside conflict by focusing on all the things you need to do, all the obligations you must meet. It won't work. Resistance, as discussed in chapter 1, makes anxiety worse.

Think for a moment about where in your body and mind you feel your stress. What chronic ache or pain or symptom shows up for you when you have too much to do? What is impacted? Your sleep, your appetite, your patience, your back, your libido, your head? Your relationships? I challenge you to honestly examine how and if being busy makes you feel better. Better in what way?

BUSY OR STILL? DON'T GO GLOBAL

If you live a life of busyness, global all-or-nothing thinking is likely a prominent pattern for you. When I talk about "stillness," you reflexively respond with, "I don't have time to meditate!" or "How can I possibly *empty* my mind?" I completely understand. I recently saw a suggestion that we spend an hour at the beginning of each day contemplating, staying off any devices, being still. *An hour?* I sneered. That's too much for me, honestly. But can I do three minutes? Five? Can you?

I don't have to do a ninety-minute yoga class, but I can do a ten-minute yoga video a few times a week. Or I can walk through my town, absorbed in a provoking or funny podcast, thinking thoughts, accountable to no one. Sometimes I cover the miles in silence while I let my creativity wander, my emotions meander. Stillness for me is active, as paradoxical as that sounds. I come up with many ideas while I'm walking or hiking. And sometimes I cry a little, for all sorts of reasons or no reason at all. The opposite of busyness is not nothingness. And stillness does not mean immobile.

The goal is not to live the life of a Buddhist monk. Being productive and even busy is fine and necessary, especially if you have a career and children and parents and fun activities. But if you treat your daily tasks like an emergency, moving from one crisis to the next, you may be a cultivator of chaos. If you live your life as if you are on the bomb squad, trying to determine if you should clip the red wire or the blue wire as the seconds tick down, you may be a cultivator of chaos.

Busyness has a way of selling itself as both necessary and out of your control. Does your anxiety demand you stay busy, while you tell yourself it's your busy life that keeps you anxious? It's a paradox you can't resolve—until you allow yourself the space to do so. This busyness doesn't just *happen to you*. You have a major role to play here as the witting or unwitting instigator in your life. Let's actively and productively address the busyness, build some skills, and change it up.

WHAT TO DO

Ask the Hard Questions (and Listen to the Answers)

If you see yourself in this chapter, it's time to ask yourself, and those close to you, some tough and vulnerable questions. And please listen to the responses you get! I find that when people get feedback about the impact of their busyness, they are quick to nod and agree but then are very unlikely to do anything about it. As you ask and get answers to these questions, notice your initial agreement because it feels validating ("Thank you for noticing how busy I am!"), and then your possible dismissal that anything can change ("But there's really nothing I can do about it").

Ask your trusted family members and friends the following hard questions. Tell them why you're asking and that you value their honest responses. If you boast or complain frequently about your hectic busy life but then have done nothing to change it, others may have learned to nod and agree but keep their genuine opinions to themselves. They'll need to know this is a different kind of conversation.

- How does my or our busyness impact you? How do you feel when I take on something else?
- What obligations would you like me (and you) to let go of?
- How often do I complain about how busy and stressed I am?
- Do you see this as a part of our family's identity? How have you taken on this way of life?
- How are your busyness and stress tied to your sense of worth?
- What changes do you predict in our family when the busyness decreases? What will feel better?
- Do I listen to you when you tell me you are overwhelmed? How do I respond?
- Do messages of busyness come from other places? Where do you hear it the most?

Then ask yourself the following questions:

- What feels good about this pattern? What's enticing about it?
- How do you promote this aspect of yourself as part of your identity? Do you use social media to humblebrag about your busyness? How do you respond when others do the same?
- Who supports this pattern? Who benefits from it?
- How do you justify its impact on yourself and others? What's the price you and others pay for your busyness?
- Do you talk and complain about your busy life, even seek advice about it, but then do nothing to change it?

- How do you dismiss the feedback you receive? How do you make the feedback not apply to you?

And if you are a parent, I urge you to talk directly to your children and teens right away. In the last decade, this pattern of busyness has worked its way down into adolescence and even into early childhood, as evidenced by the increases in anxiety and depression in these age groups. Children need your support, permission, and role modeling around "free" time. Many kids raised in overscheduled environments don't know how to play creatively or entertain themselves without screens.

When I talk to anxious families, parents often tell me that their overscheduled weekends with the kids are the worst. The days are packed with errands and activities and work; the parents want to slow down and coast a bit. But simultaneously their children cannot handle unstructured time. "We've been trying to do less," one parent of a ten-year-old told me. "But she needs to have a schedule . . . to know exactly what the day looks like, or she gets so uptight. She asks over and over what we're doing, or when we're leaving." For this family and many others, the rushing feels normal. Stillness or unstructured play—without devices—feels uncomfortable, agitating, unmoored.

It helps to acknowledge the dilemma of wanting to pack the days full but knowing the strain it causes. Ask family members when and how they find stillness or contentment. If this is a new approach for you and your family, emphasize that small doses of stillness count so that it *doesn't feel all-or-nothing or overwhelming*. Find out what they imagine changing and what they need from you to make it happen. Ask family members, "When do you feel most rushed? How do I contribute to that? If you had a chunk of time with no scheduled activities and no screens available, what would you do?"

Learn How to Say No and When to Say Yes

In the first episode of the show *Friends*, Joey asks Phoebe to help put furniture together. "Oh, I wish I could, but I don't want to," she says. Fabulous.

The most important, concrete change to make if you are trapped in busyness is saying no. Sounds simple enough. But as the old saying goes, if it were that simple, everyone would do it. Saying no effectively involves a few critical steps, just as learning to make a pie crust or parallel park as a new driver involves a combination of steps or skills. And if busyness is a valued part of your identity, you're going to be creating some new pathways in your brain. This takes practice.

If you tend to say yes too quickly—even when you know you want to say no—here are the key tips to break the cycles of the "automatic yes" and the "guilt-ridden yes":

- *Buy yourself some time.* Have a few stock responses to pull out when someone asks for something and you need to think it over. "What a kind invitation . . . I need to check my schedule," or, "I'll get back to you on that," are great. Screen your calls so that you can hear a request first and not feel pressured in the moment. Take your time before responding to a text or email. That's allowed.

- *Before you say yes, practice some future thinking and regret prevention.* Imagine what it will be like when the day of the event or task or job arrives. How will you feel then? A few years ago, a very nice organization asked me in February to do an event on a Sunday afternoon in May. I felt immediately, automatically obligated to say yes. It was a worthy cause, and I certainly didn't have anything specific planned for that Sunday so far away. My husband suggested I imagine, for a moment, that Sunday in May when the weather was finally nice in New Hampshire and the mountains were calling. I also knew the next few months were already fully booked. I'd be tired. "If you agree to do it now, then no complaining when the date arrives," he said. "Regret prevention happens ahead of time." I could clearly imagine complaining in May because I already knew that I wanted to say no. I said no.

- *Say yes sometimes.* There are times when, for good reason, we say yes to things we don't want to do. Again, it's not all-or-nothing. It's the repeated, reflexive, obligatory yes that we're trying to banish here. Create a small list of criteria to guide your acceptances. Are there a few people who depend on you for help? Do you sometimes need to make money? Do you enjoy the activity? The criteria can be somewhat flexible if the result is a combination of yeses and nos.
- *Have a few standard "no" responses at the ready.* Keep it short and polite. The biggest mistake people make when saying no is a compulsion to explain their decision, to give all sorts of details. I stole the phrase "I'm sorry, that doesn't work for me" from a friend. It changed my life.
- *Be ready for the blowback.* When you say no, people react in a variety of ways. Some express understanding, and some will be pissed. Some will express understanding to your face and be pissed behind your back. What skills do you need to develop? The ability to tolerate not knowing exactly how people feel about your no and—perhaps even trickier—tolerating their disappointment or disapproval when they share it directly. They are allowed to feel that way, and you are still allowed to say no. Remember Colton from chapter 4, who was overly accommodating in order to avoid conflict? If your busyness

pattern persists as a way to avoid conflict, then disappointing someone as you make better choices is a sign of progress, as weird as that sounds.

- *You must also tolerate the change in both your do-it-all status with others and how you define your own self-worth.* Are you known as the person who can get everything done? Do people express their amazement at how busy you are? This recognition feels like a boost, a drug for the workaholic. Perhaps it's been your goal to be seen in that light and get that little shot of approval. Your new goal is to decrease how often you define yourself as busy and stressed. Pay attention to your reply when people ask, "How are you?" Write down four genuine responses that shift the tone. "I've really been enjoying _____," or, "I stepped away from _______, and it was a good decision." Look at your social media posts; better yet, step away from social media entirely. Stop the "crazy-busy" humblebrags. (You'll now notice how often others define themselves that way. It's rampant!)

Pay Attention to Multitasking

This can be a hard habit to break, but I hope the compelling research on task switching and its inefficiency inspires you. Ultimately, busyness is more about *feeling* busy and valued than actually *being* productive. Our devices are seductive. Expecting yourself to not check email or pay attention to incoming notifications is often asking too much. When I write, I usually turn off my WiFi but not always. Those texts are fun! Those emails are important! Let's see who got kicked off Twitter! But I know when I set those limits, it makes a positive difference. I get a lot more accomplished. Keep making those adjustments.

And please share this information with the young people in your life. Even though classes on multitasking are no longer a part of business training, many young people I talk to still believe that they can divide their attention with no negative effect, or even in ways that they think help their productivity. It reminds me of the argument people make for being better drivers when buzzed. (Yes, that's a thing. It resulted in the ad campaign that clarifies, "Buzzed driving is drunk driving.") The amount of people texting and driving shows how irrational and rigid our thinking can be, and how addicted we have become to doing more, more, more—and believing we can pull it off without consequence.

Come Up with a Mantra and Keep It Short, Sweet, and Easy

I'll say it once again: Adjustments along the way are normal and necessary. You will need to make little course corrections as you notice how you "do" your busyness, so I want you to come up with a quick internal reminder that helps you *reset* when you find yourself spinning, a mental "hold on a second" when you're about to say yes instead of no, an interrupter that serves as permission *from you to you* to step back from the busyness and *regroup*.

Many years ago, I was at a small training that included an opportunity to work on personal issues as well as professional challenges. I knew what I needed to address. My boys were little, and I was starting to work more after taking a few years off. I was, in fact, away from them at the training for a few days and feeling overwhelmed by my career, their needs, and my obligations. I knew rationally that I needed to set some limits if I was going to manage better. But saying no (to adults, not my kids) was hard, especially when someone pushed for a yes and I felt guilty for refusing.

"Sounds like you need to put your foot down," a colleague suggested. So that's what we decided I'd do. When I was on the phone fielding a request (this was before texting, so the conversations were likely on the phone), I literally put my foot down. Stamped my foot like a stubborn child or an angry horse. The requester on the phone didn't hear it or see it, but I felt it. It was a signal to me. And as silly as it sounds, it connected me to the valuable insight offered at the training and the permission I'd received there to say no.

You might also come up with a word or phrase that serves as your mantra, your reminder. Keep it simple. It's your in-the-moment shortcut, not a lecture. You'll remember in chapter 2, on catastrophizing, I told you to talk 85 percent less, to lose the safety chatter. Same rules apply here, only more so. Let's bump that up to 95 percent less.

Buddha said, "Better than a thousand hollow words is one word that brings peace."

What's your word or phrase? What comes up for you?

My current favorites: *This is not an emergency*, or sometimes simply, *Reboot.* Feel free to borrow these and change them when something better pops up.

Now take five slow, full breaths, and on each exhale, repeat your word or phrase.

Go ahead. I'll wait. Oh, I'm sorry. Does that request irritate you? Do it anyway. And the next chapter on irritability will be particularly helpful.

QUESTIONS FOR PONDERING AND JOURNALING
This chapter is full of questions, so go back and review. Here are a few more to consider:
What obligations would you like to let go of?
What activities do you truly enjoy doing, and which are sheer obligational drudgery?
Who will judge you harshest for changing your pattern of busyness? Who won't?
What can you predict you will notice first when you start to move out of this pattern?
What will be a more long-term benefit that will appear over time?

CHAPTER SIX

IRRITABILITY PLAYS THE BLAME GAME

Sneaky Pattern: How Irritability Likes to Blame Others but Can Be a Red Flag for You

If we are irritated by every rub, how will we be polished?

—Rumi

I hope you've had some lightbulb moments as you read the previous chapters, some new awareness of how certain patterns or habits fuel anxiety or worry.

Wait, that's how I stay anxious?

So ruminating is not problem solving?

Yikes, my whole family is catastrophic. . . . I'm the legacy of my great-grandmother?

But irritability, I can confidently state, is not a mystery to any of us, especially after the last few years. Even in the best of times, irritability is a normal and frequent thing to experience. During tough times, feeling easily annoyed, impatient, and grumpy can seem constant. In this chapter, I do not endeavor to teach you what irritability is. I think you know. But I do offer some insight into the connection between day-to-day irritability, anxiety, and stress. I talk a bit about the risks associated with chronic irritability. Most importantly, I provide some help in reducing this common pattern.

WHEN RESEARCHERS TALK ABOUT IRRITABILITY

A surprising amount of research exists on irritability, mainly because chronic irritability is connected to a range of disorders, including anxiety and depression. Researchers examine specific components of human emotion and behavior in a quest to find causes, make correlations, and offer predictions. Are you depressed because you're more prone to anger, or is irritability a side effect of depression? How does the level of irritability in children predict future problems? How do parents react to irritable children and vice versa? Does irritability run in families?

Sometimes I find the data illuminating and helpful to my practice. Other times I wonder if researchers spend any time at all with tired parents, burned-out nurses, or neglected children. The language that researchers use can sound so detached from real-life human experience that it reminds me of studying poetry in college, pulling apart each word and phrase until the broader emotional experience was lost. With that disclaimer, I briefly offer you what current research says about irritability.

The word *irritability* is defined as being prone to anger and having the ability to *sustain that anger*. It is described clinically as an expression of frustrative nonreward, a reaction to blocked goal attainment. For example, when my car wouldn't start on a frigid winter morning, making me late for an important appointment, I had a complete and full-body reaction to blocked goal attainment. Can you relate?

Severe irritability can escalate, leading to angry outbursts, rage, and sometimes aggression. Less than 3 percent of people have this level of irritability, often referred to in the real world as having a "bad temper." Much more commonly, a chronic internal state of irritability is experienced by others as complaining, stewing, or grumpiness. Chronically irritated people are more sensitive and "touchy," which makes addressing their irritation in relationships a vicious cycle. Telling a highly irritable person to be less grumpy just makes them more irritated. And grumpy. You get nowhere.

Irritability that comes and goes is common, which leads some researchers to warn about the overpathologizing of normal irritability. While it is a prominent component of many disorders, including anxiety, depression, substance use, and trauma-related struggles, irritability is also a part of daily life. My goal here is to address the normal irritability that is part of our anxious, stressed-out culture, just as I have been addressing the common ways that anxious patterns can grab us all. That said, if you are reading this and wondering about your emotional reactivity and high level of annoyance, it might be time to recognize how dominant your irritability has become. If you or others describe you as chronically and significantly irritable to the point where it's affecting your ability to do your job, connect with others, or enjoy your life, seek help. If your angry outbursts are a regular occurrence, as compared to a *very* rare or isolated incident, and cause damage, ask for help.

THE BUZZING IN YOUR EAR

Take a moment to think about your most prominent patterns from the previous chapters and how those patterns connect or contribute to your irritability and grouchiness. How does irritability show up for you? How do you notice it in others? Do you sense it only when you are stressed about something, or is it a more simmering state of depletion? Are you too rigid with yourself and others? Are you so overscheduled and busy that your reserves are depleted? Does your worry pull you out of the present, making it hard to handle what's in front of you?

When you are in your head, overestimating a problem or overthinking an obstacle, it doesn't take much more to arrive at annoyed and cranky.

My friend described to me the connection between her "low-grade fretting"—about her grown children's employment struggles, her mother's vaccination status, among other things—and her shortness with her husband. She recently snapped at him while discussing the slippery, icy sections of their driveway. He wasn't hearing her, and she had no room for his perceived dismissal. "Relax," he told her. That didn't go over well.

I love the phrase "low-grade fretting" because this level of worry and the irritability that comes with it are not about panic or emergencies. We are most often irritable when, day after day, we are trapped in the internal anxious patterns that exhaust and disconnect us, and at the same time need to manage the ongoing life obstacles (like icy driveways) that wear us down. Irritability is not the emotional, panicked response to killer wasps; it's the simmering response to the constant buzz of a mosquito. If you've ever had a mosquito in your bedroom at night, you know how consuming it can be. Five mosquitoes, and you feel like you're losing your mind.

ANXIETY RESENTS BEING INTERRUPTED

Every anxious pattern—from ruminating to catastrophizing to creating busyness—demands our attention. They don't like to be interrupted. When we are inside, doing our worry thing, we have little room for much else. Predictably, when our anxious patterns are interrupted, we feel irritated and snap back. A woman once described to me what it was like to fly with her very anxious husband. As the plane began to take off, she asked him a question, nothing important. "Don't talk to me!" he sniped. "I'm keeping the plane in the air!" He was completely absorbed in his catastrophic thinking, performing whatever internal rituals he needed to do to calm and protect himself, and apparently all other passengers as well.

I had a client many years ago who was constantly irritated with her adult children. They always cut her off, she said, ending phone calls abruptly or sometimes changing the subject in the middle of a conversation. "Ask them why they do that," I told her. "Tell them you want an honest answer." I suspected I already knew the answer.

In my office she would routinely veer off on tangents about terrible things that had happened to other people she barely knew from her church or small town. Her recounting of catastrophic events was hard to stop, even when I pointed out that they had little to do with her.

Angrily she once said to me, "Well, perhaps you'd think otherwise if you ever let me finish." I understood that her ruminating felt protective, as if she could prevent bad things from happening to her family by repeatedly examining those tragedies. She didn't share my view. Because her children and I were unwilling to join in her ruminating, we stood as irritating obstacles to her pattern. She wanted to ruminate and demanded an attentive audience.

Repetitive negative thinkers are irritated by interruptions because they confuse the imagining of worst-case scenarios with problem solving. They want to run through the possibilities as a way to protect and prevent. One friend humorously named a part of her husband "Travel Dad." Travel Dad shows up, not surprisingly, a few days before any family outing. He is tense and a bit demanding as he runs through every possible outcome, either out loud to family members or in his head. The kids joke about it, she told me. "No one talks to Travel Dad. He's unavailable for comment while he goes over the details of the fiery car crash or bed bug infestation." They know he will be irritable, and they don't take it personally, although he blames them for his snappiness. He sees any interruptions as disrespectful, pulling him away from the focus that his worry demands. "You joke all you want," he says. "But I'm the responsible one here."

She doubts he'll ever be able to acknowledge his catastrophic worrying or own his reactions to others. Luckily, the family has learned how to handle it with humor. They don't feel the sting of his blaming, although this is not the norm in many families.

LITTLE WIGGLE ROOM, BIG IRRITATION

Perfectionism cannot exist without irritation. People with patterns of perfectionism, trapped in their black-and-white rigidity, feel irritated with themselves and others for not meeting the highest of standards. If you are to successfully meet the demands of your global, perfectionistic part, then others must stay out of your way or cooperate fully. This is hard to achieve, as we discussed in chapter 3. You—and those around you—will all pay a price.

How often do you feel irritated because someone is interrupting your perfect plan? Messing up your rigid schedule? Of course, we all feel irritated when something gets screwed up, but these feelings should come and go. They should be directed at a specific situation rather than spread widely around, aimed indiscriminately at people who don't deserve it. The more rigid and perfectionistic you are, the more this type of irritability becomes a way of life. It's a constant internal battle you fight with yourself and an external clash with our imperfect world and the imperfect, incompetent people who occupy it.

A house across the street from my gym is shockingly perfect. Honestly, I've never seen anything like it. The symmetry of the curtains in the windows. The edging of the flower gardens with tulips planted in symmetrical rows. Never a speck of *anything* on the perfectly sealed black driveway. One warm Saturday morning, a bunch of us took our workout outside into the parking lot. It was close to nine o'clock and we were adults, behaving like adults.

Soon after we started, the owner of the perfect house emerged and walked quickly across the street to ask if we had permission to be there. Was this to be a regular occurrence? How many people would be attending? I'd never met her before, but to be honest, she interacted with us just as I would have predicted. Whenever I go by the house, I truly think to myself, *That must be exhausting.* And here she was, with her exhaustion and control and irritability now spilling over onto a group of people across the street. Somehow, we were interfering with her perfect plan or perhaps simply being too loud and unpredictable. She was rigid and touchy and grumpy. Here she was, *angry and able to sustain that anger.*

The same goes for the overscheduled people-pleasers and those trapped in busyness. Without belaboring the point, hear this: if you have cultivated a life of created chaos—not out of necessity, but for the reasons I laid out in the previous chapter—you will be irritable.

AND ALSO, SOMETIMES LIFE SUCKS

Constant, simmering irritability is the result of many factors; but to be clear, it's often the symptom, not the source. Whatever the cause, it's an exhausting place to be. And as justifiable as it may be—as valid as it may be—you need to heed its warning. It's a red flag, the check-engine light. Hopefully, the previous chapters have helped you identify your anxious patterns so that you can now take action to escape them. Tackle the source to decrease your irritability. Where do you need to say no? Where do you need to set boundaries? Are you creating a narrative in your head that's making life feel scary or anxiety provoking?

Finally, I want to announce, loud and clear, that you might be irritable because the last few years have been terrible. I wrote this book to help you look at your patterns and uncover how anxiety grabs hold. People have limited perceptions of anxiety and misunderstand it—or just plain miss it and get it wrong—so I'm here to clarify. But sometimes we're just worn out. The ongoing impact of the pandemic, social and racial inequities, the opioid crisis, the mental health of our children, brutal war, concerns about the environment— have depleted us. Sometimes we do get locked into anxious patterns that absolutely add to our irritability. Sometimes irritation shows up because life really is hard.

As always, we're not going to eliminate irritation, just as we're not going to eliminate worry or sadness or anger or grief. It'll show up because you're a human, and life includes suffering. In addition to all the tips offered in the previous chapters—all the things you've already started to do differently—here are a few more concrete ways to help with your irritability, no matter why or how it arrived.

WHAT TO DO

Own It

It's not fun to be irritable, and it's equally not fun to be around people who are irritable. What makes it worse is when you, the irritable person, blame everyone else for your impatience and crankiness. You will be irritable at times. You're tired. Your furnace needs to be replaced. Your toddler found your favorite lipstick and colored his entire face with it, including the inner folds of his nostrils and ears. (True story.) You're trying to loosen up your perfectionism—and you're doing great!—but your daughter's messy room is driving you nuts.

So own it. Come clean. Announce to whoever needs to hear it that you are running on fumes or simply having a rough day. When appropriate, tell them why. I talked earlier about being open with your family when you go global, asking for a redo. The same concept applies here.

Irritability is normal. Blame is corrosive. None of us can possibly be happy all the time. We're often irritated by things that we didn't want or cause. But you should not expect those around you to take responsibility for your bad days, especially if they are the result of your unmanaged or unacknowledged anxiety.

Again these last several years have taken a toll. "The world is too much with us," wrote poet William Wordsworth in 1802, mourning man's disconnection from nature. What would he think now? If you are finding yourself being more irritable than normal, if you feel exhausted and have little patience, you are not alone. Pay attention. Be open with others. Talk to your family about the fact that you are working on it. If you know you are irritable, tell them so. "I apologize. I feel like I've been so cranky the last few days. I'm working on that." Simple and genuine statements can change the dynamic of your relationships and can interrupt toxic patterns in ways you might not predict.

My office is attached to my house. I can be in there for hours and hours. Maybe I'm doing presentations or seeing clients or writing. When I walk back into my house, I often say to my family, "I apologize ahead of time. I've got nothing left. So if I'm quiet, if I'm short, if I'm a little cranky, it has nothing to do with you. I'm just tapped out. Give me a few minutes."

Check In, Keep It Simple, Start Early

Edith was a tax accountant who came to see me at the end of an exhausting tax season. She worked for one of those large, franchised tax service companies. As an avowed perfectionist, she reveled in the precision of numbers and the solving of tax puzzles, but the expectations for volume were high and not every customer was friendly nor appreciative. I assumed the job was the source of her stress, the reason for her appointment, so when I asked her if she ever considered leaving the company, her response surprised me. "Oh no, please, I can handle the stress of my job. It's really only awful for two, maybe three months of the year. But I need my daughter to handle it, too." Edith was a single mother, and the conflict with her fifteen-year-old daughter, Ada, was what brought her in. Edith was a concrete thinker. Job was job; home was home. "I have good boundaries. I don't bring work home. But when I come through the door, I want to leave the day behind. I see dishes in the sink, and my daughter is on her phone. I just want to relax, but she infuriates me."

I asked Edith to bring Ada to a session. Listening to them together, the description of their pattern was predictable. From late February through mid-April, they had the same argument over and over. Edith came home, surveyed the scene, and then barked at Ada to do her share. Ada snapped back, accusing Edith of overreacting. "I do so much around here! Don't blame me because your job sucks!" Edith denied her job was the issue, blaming her crankiness on Ada. "We wouldn't argue if you did what I asked you to do," she yelled.

"We wouldn't fight if you didn't come through the door like a witch!" Ada yelled back.

Sometimes my job is challenging. This was not one of those times. The three of us quickly framed up the problem. Their conflicts erupted when they were both most irritable. Edith, despite her best efforts and admirable boundaries, was in fact often drained from her demanding days. For a perfectionist, the house looking perfect felt *good and necessary*, so she felt angry when she walked into any mess at all. Ada, it turned out, had long days, too. She was a solid student with an independence that served her well as the only child of a very hard-working mother. Being bossed around was the last thing she felt she deserved after responsibly managing herself all day at school. She wanted to shut down, disconnect, space out.

We decided a simple check-in was required when they first came together at the end of the day. We used a 1–10 irritability scale, 1 representing completely chill and content, 10 highly irritable, worn out, on edge. Edith needed to learn to take a moment and honestly assess her irritation level before she walked in the door, a new skill that she was willing to take on. "You can successfully leave work at work and still carry some of the emotional stench home with you," I told her. "If you worked on a farm, you'd come home smelling like cows and dirt." Edith would walk in and say something like, "Hi Ada, I'm home. Feeling like a 7 right now . . . pretty worn out." Ada would then reply, "Understood! I'm a 2. Feeling psyched that I finished my science project."

This simple scale and these two-minute conversations, I hoped, would pave the way for longer conversations too. Ada would benefit from paying attention to her own emotional and physical state as well. What did she need when she was spiraling up at an 8 or a 9? Could she let Edith know? How will she stay connected to what works for her while she stays connected to those she cares about? Their communication didn't need to be, as Ada put it, "all touchy-feely and creepy." We found a way to practice directness and openness, which is good relationship modeling for this high-achieving teen as she heads into the world. When mother and daughter owned their irritability and stopped the blaming, the bickering decreased in a flash.

Several times in this chapter and throughout the book, I have talked about the need to reset, to rejuvenate, to step away from patterns. Sometimes it's as quick as a few slow breaths, as simple as a walk in the sunshine, or as intoxicating as a solid night's sleep. A participant in one of our workshops offered the mantra "A little space offers you grace."

Breaths, mantras, walks, talks. We can't discuss anxiety without mentioning self-care. I know, "self-care" is a buzzword used so often of late that it has become almost meaningless because it can mean almost anything. So what is self-care, really? And more importantly, what is it *not*? An important distinction is to be made, and that's the challenge of our final chapter.

QUESTIONS FOR PONDERING AND JOURNALING
How do you feel when you're on the receiving end of irritability?
What are your go-to mood changers? What about your partner's or children's?
Some people take on irritability as their persona and expect others to allow for that. ("This is just who I am. Deal with it.") Do you know anyone like that?
Where do you need to say "no"? Where do you need to set boundaries?
How likely are you to blame others or situations for your irritability?

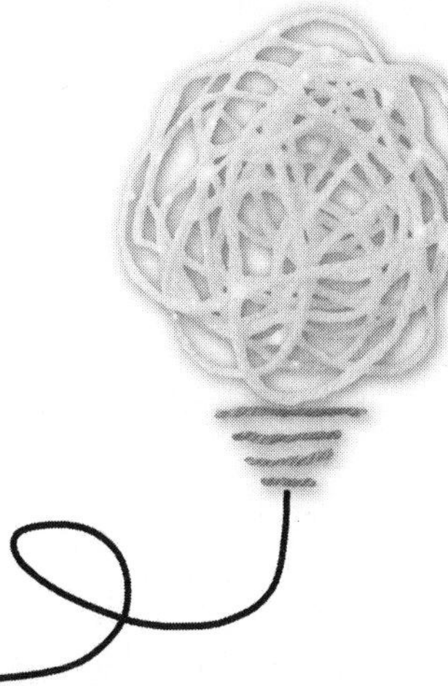

CHAPTER SEVEN

HOW SELF-CARE GOES AWRY

Sneaky Pattern: How Self-Care Is Hijacked and Becomes Not Self-Care at All

Most of the shadows of this life are caused by standing in one's own sunshine.

—Ralph Waldo Emerson

What is self-care? How do you define it? Are you sick of hearing about it?

All the previous chapters are full of suggestions for self-care. When you interrupt the patterns that add to your anxiety, you're taking care of yourself. When you move out of busyness, when you unhook yourself from your repetitive negative thinking, when you take steps to acknowledge and shift out of irritability, when you have a tough but important conversation with your partner about household responsibilities—all that's self-care. Additionally, many concrete things you do are relaxing or rejuvenating or productive, whether painting or walking with your dog or reading a novel before bed.

Of course, what I find most relaxing and rejuvenating may not be what you find most rejuvenating. I remember going on a girls' weekend decades ago, and some friends wanted to stop at the big-box store that specializes in 24/7 Christmas. Stick a needle in my eye. I went, of course, but not on my list. You get to determine what works for you. It's personal.

Well, sort of. But not entirely.

Ironically, self-care isn't just about you. Calling it self-care, in fact, is a rather inaccurate label because it so directly involves and impacts those in your orbit. It's relational because when you don't take care of yourself, others pay a price. Either they must step in and care for you (because you didn't) or people miss out on what you have to offer but can't, because you are ill, depleted, avoiding, or unavailable. Self-care supports connection—and when self-care goes awry, connection suffers, sometimes dramatically.

One goal of this chapter is to go beyond the obvious self-care suggestions, which are solid and helpful and, I fully recognize, may border on the annoying at this point. I hope to offer some interesting new information about what you think you already know, for example, how sleep and exercise impact your mood, your thinking, and your anxiety. Then I'll talk about how self-care slides off-course; how, with the best of intentions, your self-care plan doesn't help or even makes your life more anxious or stressful. The final sneaky ways that anxiety grabs hold include:

- Using "self-care" as a crutch to avoid
- Allowing self-care practices to morph into rigidity and control
- Disguising or misidentifying self-medication as self-care

IS IT SELF-CARE OR SELF-MEDICATION, AND WHY SHOULD I CARE?

What do we mean by "self-medication"? It certainly includes the use of actual medication and other substances to feel better, but more broadly, it includes anything that offers an in-the-moment escape or avoidance. Just like using procrastination to cope with anxiety, the immediate sensation is relief, but the long-term result increases the problem. Some use the term *self-medication* in a positive way, seeing it as the act of taking steps to care for yourself. I am not using it in this way. For the sake of consistency and clarity, I'm making a clear distinction between the two, and here's how I know the difference: when I am practicing self-care, I rarely if ever feel regret or shame afterward. Self-medication, however, often leads to regret. True self-care does not have negative consequences for you or those you care about. Self-medication often does. Self-medication feels like a reward but isn't truly rewarding.

In this anxious world of ours, I have noticed the distinction between the two becoming increasingly blurred and confusing. Like what I described in chapter 1 with ruminating disguising itself as problem solving, I increasingly see people confusing self-medication with self-care. You might be doing something that reduces your immediate anxiety or worry, but this short-term goal of elimination or avoidance makes your functioning worse over time.

Any substance or behavior can be used to self-medicate: to numb out, avoid, or distract from what truly needs attention. That substance or behavior can be anything from alcohol to chocolate to pornography to lottery tickets to exercise. I'm going to focus on the common manners in which self-care has lost its way, appearing to work the "best" to help our anxiety, but in reality serving to increase it, sometimes with devastating outcomes. As you work to uncover your own patterns, the main questions to ask are these: *Am I using this substance or behavior to escape or eliminate my feelings or worries in the short term? How is it working in the long term?*

SLEEP, SELF-CARE, AND SELF-MEDICATION: IT'S KIND OF A MESS

"I never have any time to myself," says thirty-four-year-old Leah. The divorced mother of six-year-old twins works full time and is active in local politics. She's exhausted and irritable, and often has difficulty sleeping. Even when she does meet her goal of seven hours, she still feels "like a zombie" most days. Her doctor gave her a prescription of Ambien to use as needed, and she takes the medication sporadically and with hesitation. "I've got two little kids. I can't be out cold at night," she says. "But I'm desperate sometimes."

Each night, she gets the twins in bed by eight o'clock and then usually drifts off with them as they read or snuggle. Waking about an hour later, she picks up the house and prepares for the next morning, then finally climbs into her bed with her laptop to relax with Netflix. "This is my treat, my time alone," she says. She turns her computer off around eleven, knowing she must get up by five the next morning, but often tosses and turns until past midnight.

Leah's story is typical. The self-care she wants and deserves at the end of her day *sounds* good, but the short-term pleasure of staying up late and using a screen in bed are creating long-term problems. Is watching Netflix always self-medication? Of course not. But denying herself adequate sleep to get the "reward" of alone time is backfiring. When the alarm goes off at 5 a.m., Leah regrets staying up too late. When she is irritable with her children and unfocused at work, she vows to fix the problem. So she goes to her doctor, complains of difficulty sleeping, and leaves with a prescription. Taking a sleeping medication (which she and many others in the same situation choose to do) becomes part of the self-medication approach. Does she add caffeine to the mix? Likely, and that extra cup of coffee she craves becomes another "reward" that she has earned. Ah, that first cup of coffee in the morning.

Look, I get it. I watch Netflix too. On days when I'm scheduled to the minute, I can't wait to simply sit and be entertained. And I love coffee. With caffeine. When my boys were little, I sacrificed sleep for alone time. I wanted solitude, and I wanted to be awake during the solitude. I told myself it was what I needed. Exhaustion was the price I was willing to pay. More than once I came to regret this backward thinking, but probably not enough. Do I still at times stay awake too late when I know I have an early day? Yes, but very infrequently. I am much more honest with myself about the price I pay and the regret I will feel.

And let me talk for a moment about screens.

When my boys were little, "screens at night" meant my husband and I renting DVDs of *The Sopranos* and watching several episodes in a row on our television. We stayed up too late, but it felt like a treat —until our little boys woke us at sunrise. Twenty years later, those

LED screens are in beds and in hands, inches from people's eyeballs. This is confusing our primitive brain's circuitry.

Human beings are regulated by potent and primitive interactions between our eyes and our brains, light and darkness. We are ruled by our circadian rhythms because it's literally how the world works: the movement between day and night. Light hitting our retina resets our master sleep clock; the systems in our eyes and brains that regulate our wakefulness and sleepiness are powerful. Light at night interferes with sleep onset, the natural release of melatonin, and next-morning alertness. As much as we try, these primary systems will not be fooled. We are designed to be awake when it's light and asleep when it's dark.

Smartphone use at night impacts sleep, but exactly what's at play remains up for some debate. One factor is the blue light emitted by their screens, but another may also be its entertaining character or related psychological effects, or both. And whether or not the "night shift" mode that reduces blue light has any significant impact on the circadian system is still being researched. A study done in 2021 looked at phone use before bed and found that the blue light didn't help—but it was not the only factor delaying sleep onset. "While there is a lot of evidence suggesting that blue light increases alertness and makes it more difficult to fall asleep, it is important to think about what portion of that stimulation is light emission versus other cognitive and psychological stimulations," said researcher Chad Jensen in an interview for the website Technology Networks.

Much of the research on the impacts of sleep deprivation and screens has focused on teens and young adults. Multiple studies find clear connections between sleep deprivation and access to screens. Screens in bedrooms and engagement with social media at night correlate with sleep problems and depression symptoms in teens, and refusal to act on this very clear information underscores their allure, their addictive qualities.

Do we think these behaviors don't impact adults as well? How long ago were you a teen? And what habits have persisted or developed in adulthood? How are you justifying and allowing these patterns to control you and your family? If it's destructive to your child or teen, how can it be deemed self-care for you?

If your "self-care" is really a way to compensate for an actual lack of self-care, it's not self-care. Adequate sleep is good self-care. Denying yourself sleep and calling it a reward, then trying to compensate for the lack of sleep with substances is self-medicating.

If you are anxious, irritable, stressed out, and generally feeling crappy, sleep needs to be high on the list of your self-care priorities. Research has shown over and over that despite our best efforts at justifications and rationalizations, our brains and bodies want adequate sleep and suffer when we don't get it. A study that Yvonne Harris and James Horne led in 1999 found that even after one night of sleep deprivation, people were more rigid in their thinking, made more perseverative errors, and had difficulty adjusting to updated information or situations. Other researchers have found that without adequate sleep, we are less empathetic, more sensitive to pain, and less aware that we are even having cognitive difficulty. Like a toddler melting down because she needs a nap, we are often unaware of the impact of our tiredness.

In chapter 1, I talked about how anxiety and depression disrupt sleep, and described the alphabet game, my go-to for unhooking from the pattern of repetitive negative thinking. I also talked about Cognitive Behavioral Therapy for Insomnia (CBT-I) as a way to address insomnia. If you are self-medicating to fall sleep, and then to stay awake the next day, I strongly urge you to focus on behavioral changes. Start first with examining your screen use at night. And please know that regardless of why you aren't sleeping enough, the result is the same. It goes both ways: whether you want to fall asleep but can't, or you are engaging in the conscious pattern of denying yourself sleep in the guise of self-care, you will add to your anxiety.

A COCKTAIL OF MIXED MESSAGES: ALCOHOL AND ANXIETY

"I've been noticing that my mom has been drinking more at night lately, even during the week," seventeen-year-old Serena told me recently. I'd been seeing Serena for her anxiety for a few years, and I knew her parents well. Both had demanding jobs in the public sector, and the last few years had been brutal. Her parents routinely had wine with dinner, but Serena now saw her mother pouring a glass as soon as she got home from work and having at least two or three more before the end of the night. "It's not like she's an alcoholic or anything," said Serena. "But she's way into it. It's like the best part of her day. She says if I had her job, I'd need wine, too."

Alcohol. How do you view it? What is your relationship with it? How does our culture—the big culture we inhabit and the smaller culture of our own families and social networks—accept it, promote it, and even revere it? If I were from another planet and attempted to understand this substance called alcohol, I'd be confused. I grew up right here on Earth, and I routinely find the messaging around alcohol baffling and astounding. It must be fabulous, right? It's a part of every celebration, gathering, or momentous occasion. It's advertised, fetishized, collected, glamorized, and ritualized. Yet few families escape the negative and sometimes tragic impacts of alcohol, including mine.

I don't want to sound too judgmental but—fair warning—I'm probably going to be a bit judgmental, which is to be expected based on what I do for a living and what this book and this chapter address. My judgment is not aimed at you; it's aimed at the way alcohol and other substances are promoted as the vital and often most effective solution to our hectic, anxious lives. My goal here is to help (and perhaps challenge) you to make the distinction between your patterns of self-care and self-medication in a world where addictive and damaging substances are an integral part of social gatherings, where they are viewed not only as what you need, but what you *deserve*. Like many of the sneaky tactics of anxiety I've described, these substances draw us in because they make us feel better immediately. They often reduce our anxiety and stress dramatically *in the short term*, and this is the very aspect that makes them so appealing and compelling. It's also what makes them so destructive over time. Is it really helping?

For example, take mommy wine culture, with memes and T-shirts and Etsy merchandise that often use humor, self-deprecation, and some blaming of children to justify alcohol as the reward for getting through the day. The reward? Rates of alcohol use disorder (AUD) have increased in women by 84 percent over the past ten years relative to a 35 percent increase in men.

A study released by the Rand Corporation in September 2020 reported that during the first months of the pandemic shutdown, women increased their heavy drinking episodes (defined as four or more drinks within a couple of hours) by 41 percent. The researchers conclude, "This substantive increase in female drinking is alarming, given that women experience greater alcohol-related health consequences compared to men. Stress is strongly associated with all phases of alcohol addiction, including drinking initiation, maintenance, and relapse for both women and men, but plays an especially critical role for women."

I recently saw an ad for personalized wine bottle labels being marketed as teacher gifts. The labels are "customized with a picture (of *your* child, please note!) and two lines of text." "Your child may be the reason they drink, so let them know how much you appreciate everything they do with our *humorous and light-hearted* The Reason You Drink Personalized Wine Bottle Label, attached to a nice bottle of wine!" said the ad (italics theirs, not mine).

I am not going to globally say that consuming alcohol is bad, but I would never include it on a list of self-care strategies. You may want to take stock right now of how many people alcohol may have damaged or at least adversely affected in your larger family or circle of acquaintances. If you tend toward anxiety or depression, using alcohol as a way to manage your symptoms or your mood is dangerous. Researchers have found that anxious people who report using alcohol to self-medicate are much more likely to develop alcohol dependence. And those who hold higher expectancies for alcohol to be anxiety-reducing are at even greater risk. We need to acknowledge the trap of alcohol and anxiety: that a drink can take the edge off a hard day yet add to one's problems the next.

Finally, we can add sleep into the mix. Studies have long demonstrated that alcohol taken in low-to-moderate doses initially promotes sleep, although this "put-you-to-sleep" effect wears off within a few days of nightly use. You may at first fall asleep quicker, but alcohol impairs your ability to stay asleep and disrupts the necessary deep

REM sleep, even in light or occasional drinkers. You will fall asleep quicker, but you will not stay asleep, and the sleep you do get will not be restorative.

The messages that promote alcohol as reward and a celebrated part of social connection are ubiquitous. The pandemic didn't help, as the lines blurred between self-care and self-medication, between reward and regret. Serena's mother was on a slippery slope, and Serena was picking up on the very patterns that lead to long-term struggles.

In short, believing that alcohol is a way to manage anxiety or stress, and viewing it as *helpful* drastically increases multiple problems. People with anxiety disorders who reported drinking to cope with their symptoms had a fivefold increased risk for developing alcohol dependence within three years. It's important to consider how you are using alcohol. If you view it as a way to manage your anxiety, endorsing it as your go-to, you are at significant risk.

CBD AND THC AND ANXIETY

Like alcohol, marijuana is widely used recreationally. Unlike alcohol, it has also been given medical status, being used to successfully treat glaucoma, nausea due to cancer treatment, pain, and other serious conditions, and in this category it has been helpful to many. It's also become the drug of choice for many dealing with anxiety and insomnia, hailed as the solution without side effects, the risk-free way to improve your mental well-being. But is it?

Research about the use of cannabis for mental health issues is still in its infancy, based on how researchers investigate and make conclusions about such things. But what about your own personal research? How and why you use cannabis, and how you classify its role in your life will be led by the same questions I laid out for alcohol use. I fully acknowledge that the information can be confusing. Who and what you believe are influenced greatly by your own biases and experiences. Let me offer you some information to help with your decision-making.

First off, today's pot is not the pot of the seventies or eighties. Prior to the 1990s, the THC content (the psychoactive ingredient that makes you "high") was less than 2 percent. By 2017, the THC content in marijuana plants was 17 to 28 percent. Concentrated THC products, such as oils and gummies, are now manufactured with THC levels up to 95 percent. While lower concentrations of THC and the use of CBD (the nonpsychoactive substance present in widely available and legal oils and creams) has been found to decrease anxiety, it is the high levels of THC that can result in significant anxiety and other mental health complications, and much of what is available currently is in that higher—and thus riskier—category.

Young brains are particularly at risk, with increasing instances of psychotic episodes and suicidality in teens over the last several years. A study done in Australia followed 1,600 girls over seven years. Those using marijuana at least one time a week were twice as likely to develop depression. Those who used daily were five times more likely to develop depression and anxiety than nonusers.

Other research indicates that, at lower doses, those who were anxious before using became less anxious, but those who were not anxious at the start became more anxious. Conclusions about how and when to use cannabis to treat anxiety vary widely. In my practice, anxious clients report a range of reactions. Some feel incredibly anxious and paranoid and avoid it completely. (Those who are socially anxious tend to use alcohol more than marijuana.) Others use it nightly to fall asleep. My biggest concern is for those who use it daily, convinced that it helps them feel normal and is keeping their anxiety at bay. Anna Lembke, MD, author of *Dopamine Nation,* describes the flaw in this thinking: "Any drug that stimulates our reward pathway the way cannabis does has the potential to change our brain's baseline anxiety." The brain gets dependent upon the cannabis, so the anxiety is actually withdrawal and the cannabis relieves it, similar to what happens with other drugs like alcohol or opioids. "Cannabis," she writes, "becomes the cause of our anxiety rather than the cure." She recommends a minimum of four weeks' abstinence to reset the reward pathway. This length of abstinence is needed to determine what's really going on with the anxiety and treat it accordingly.

I do not put the use of substances in the category of self-care. That doesn't mean that by default I put *all use* into the realm of self-medication either. I know that some people drink or smoke occasionally because they enjoy it, and it's nothing more than that. Go ahead and have fun. Just don't try to convince me that substance use is good for you or your mental well-being.

Dealing with either anxiety or depression is hard enough. Adding substance use makes it worse in every domain. If you need help to clarify or address your use, seek that help. You are not alone.

ANXIETY MEDICATIONS

People often ask me about medications for anxiety. It's confusing to many people because medications classified as antidepressants (such as Zoloft and Prozac) are currently approved and often prescribed for those with anxiety, and in certain circumstances are quite helpful as an adjunct to psychotherapy. It's beyond the scope of this book for me to dive fully into this topic, but as it pertains to the topic of self-medication, there is important information you should have regarding the most commonly prescribed antianxiety medication, the class of drugs called benzodiazepines, often referred to as benzos.

Interestingly, the vast majority of people taking benzodiazepines for anxiety are taking them just as their providers have instructed, so in many cases the term *self-medication* is not wholly accurate. I include this information here because the prescription and use of benzodiazepines is controversial to say the least, based on the frequency with which they're prescribed, their overall effectiveness in treating anxiety over the long term, the harms resulting from long-term use, and a recent FDA statement and black-box warning. If my goal is to bolster your self-care and increase your awareness about how best to manage your emotional self, then I want you to be up-to-date and aware. This is important information you, your family, and friends should have to make informed decisions and best advocate for your care.

Benzodiazepines are one of the most commonly prescribed drugs in the United States and the most frequently prescribed psychotropic medication. Between 1996 and 2013, data show a 67 percent increase in adults filling benzo prescriptions. During this period, the total quantity of benzo prescriptions filled increased 3.3-fold, meaning that more people were getting more pills. Recent years have shown a downturn in this trend, but numbers remain high. In 2019, an estimated 92 million benzodiazepine prescriptions were dispensed from US outpatient pharmacies. Alprazolam (brand name Xanax) tops the list at 38 percent of prescriptions, followed by clonazepam (brand name Klonopin) at 24 percent and lorazepam (brand name Ativan) at 20 percent.

These medications are effective in helping with what is described as crisis-level anxiety. They are meant for short-term use for intense symptoms or for specific anxiety-provoking situations, such as helping the extremely fearful flyer get on that plane to their uncle's funeral. They also have other uses, including the treatment of seizures and other movement disorders. Over the last several years, more attention has been paid to the experiences of people trying to get off benzodiazepines. Withdrawal symptoms are often intense but have been historically dismissed or minimized by providers. Additionally, there has been a lack of information given to patients when the drugs were initiated, namely that dependence can occur within weeks of regular usage and that tapering must be done with great care. Even when taken as prescribed, dependence may develop after only weeks of treatment, and discontinuation produces severe withdrawal symptoms, rebound symptoms, and anxiety, making it hard to determine what's truly happening.

Despite this knowledge, data from 2018 show that an estimated 50 percent of patients who were dispensed oral benzodiazepines received them for a duration of two months or longer. Steven Wright, MD, in an informational July 2021 webinar sponsored by the US Food and Drug Administration and the Duke Margolis Center for Health Policy, stated that 80 percent of those taking benzodiazepines have been taking them for more than six months, despite no demonstrated long-term benefits for their anxiety. Increased concern prompted the FDA to release this statement in September 2020, announcing a stronger black-box warning for these substances:

> To address the serious risks of abuse, addiction, physical dependence, and withdrawal reactions, the U.S. Food and Drug Administration (FDA) is requiring the Boxed Warning be updated for all benzodiazepine medicines.

> Benzodiazepines are widely used to treat many conditions, including anxiety, insomnia, and seizures. *The current prescribing information for benzodiazepines does not provide adequate warnings about these serious risks and harms associated with these medicines so they may be prescribed and used inappropriately.* . . . Our review found that benzodiazepines are widely prescribed and widely abused and misused in the U.S., often for long periods of time.

Research shows that successfully *withdrawing* from benzodiazepines decreases the anxiety they are meant to treat. Recommendations that benzodiazepines *not be used* as a first-line treatment for anxiety are standard. Yet prescribing these drugs remains so prevalent that even after thirty years in this business, I find it shocking. We must pay attention to how our attempts to feel less anxious can sometimes make us more dependent and more anxious.

WHEN THE LINE IS EVEN TRICKIER

Certain substances fall easily into the category of self-medication, and we can clearly see how their powerful addiction/withdrawal cycle creates and exacerbates anxiety. A teen can try to convince me that smoking pot all day is their key to success (and many have tried, believe me), but I'm not buying it. A parent can argue that nightly drinking is better than their anxious ruminating and that nothing else works, but I'll always reject this as the best or only solution.

What about the things we do that are good for us, until they're not? How do we know when self-care moves into self-medication? And can there be movement both ways between the two categories? Yes, there can be movement, and you can recognize the difference when you remember the definition I offered above: when we practice self-care, we rarely if ever feel regret. It's often not black-and-white, not all-or-nothing. Adjustments are normal and needed because it's very common to have a hobby or a favorite food or activity that provides you with joy and connection and replenishment, but then slides into self-medication—routinely or occasionally—and adds to your anxiety. How do you tell?

- When you feel regretful after the fact
- When you notice yourself becoming increasingly rigid about the activity
- When the goal of the activity is almost entirely in the category of "making you stop feeling bad" instead of making you feel replenished

Let's use exercise as a great example. Exercise or physical activity is solidly in the self-care category. Researchers consistently find exercise to be helpful for the treatment of anxiety and depression, and large studies have concluded that exercise is protective against anxiety and depression across age groups, regions, and other demographic factors. A 2021 Swedish study followed almost 400,000 cross-country skiers over twenty-one years and found that those who skied regularly had a 62 percent lower relative risk of getting diagnosed with an anxiety disorder compared to nonskiers. (The one exception was the top-performing females. The fastest women skiers did not have less anxiety.)

When rates of physical activity were assessed before and during the pandemic, more activity correlated with better mood. This is not news to any of you. And if I had to pick only one thing that I could force my anxious clients to do to help with their symptoms, I'd pick exercise.

So there we have it: exercise is good for brains, hearts, sleep, and mood. But it can move into the self-medication category, too, when it becomes a rigid or addictive pattern that adds to anxiety rather than relieves it.

Several years ago, I was working with two parents and their three children. The focus was mainly on one of the children, but everyone in the family was anxious to some degree. The mom (I'll call her Carrie) was a runner, and she talked about how it helped her anxiety tremendously. She never regretted going for a run, although she sometimes regretted missing a family event or angering her partner with her inflexibility about it. It boosted her mood and made her calmer, she said. She needed it.

All of this I easily understood because exercise is my self-care method of choice. But I began to hear her children make comments about her running, and it made me wonder if it was as "replenishing" as she reported. "If she can't go on her run, she totally loses her shit," the thirteen-year-old daughter reported in one session. Another time, "She's so much better after she runs. She paces like a caged animal before she goes."

When Carrie arrived for one session dressed in her running gear and adamantly argued that she needn't be present for the session with her daughter because she had a run planned, it was time to help her differentiate between self-care and a more addictive pattern. Running absolutely helped her anxiety. She loved it for all the right reasons, including the social connections. But she needed help being more flexible, which meant prioritizing her runs as vital self-care *and* adapting when needed. The benefits of exercising were being hijacked by her catastrophic, all-or-nothing approach.

Not being able to run for any reason became an anxiety-provoking emergency because running, she came to understand, was the only time she didn't feel anxious. This meant that much of her thinking when she was not running was worrying about what might get in the way of her run. When we looked at how her thoughts and behavior around running encompassed most of the seven anxiety patterns, she began to see how the patterns showed up in other areas of her life, too.

She was a skilled self-medicator, a darn good avoider, an expert catastrophizer, a professional ruminator. Running was absolutely a better choice than some other stuff she'd used to feel better, like spending money she didn't have on clothes. Running on the road, she joked, worked much better than running up her credit cards. And that's absolutely true. Carrie didn't want to stop running, and I wasn't even close to recommending that. Running moved more into self-care when she was able to take the patterns of anxiety—her global, catastrophic, rigid, avoidant responses—out of it.

Changing these patterns is a process, but her running now helps her anxiety far more than it adds to it. When she misses a run, she's able to handle it because her thinking has shifted from, "I must run today or I'll lose it," to, "I run as one way to improve my mood, and it's a long-term practice." She doesn't like missing a planned run, but she responds differently now. At first, she needed to remind herself of this over and over, even when her anxiety resisted believing it. It's become easier with practice. By embracing flexibility and bolstering her ability to adjust, Carrie reduced the ruminating and more fully enjoyed the benefits of her runs.

When an activity, whether it's running or drinking or shopping or cleaning, becomes a primary way to avoid, and even becomes the only way to find temporary relief, it means your self-care has become too rigid, compulsive, and anxiety-provoking. Are you rewarding yourself, or simply *trying to avoid dealing with yourself*? Or others? Self-care enhances your ability to be connected.

WHAT TO DO

Be Flexible

At times, self-care can be perceived as selfish both by you and others, which can be hard to sort out. In general, I think we successfully practice self-care by keeping a dose of flexibility handy to use as needed. Self-medicating has a rigid, internally focused feel to it, an anxious quality that I talked about in chapter 4 on inner isolation. When Carrie wanted to run instead of attending the family session, her family members saw her as self-centered. Her need to run took precedence over an important family matter, and it was clear to all of us that her anxiety and rigidity made that call. If I had refused to go into the Christmas store on that girls' weekend trip, I would have been viewed as rigid and difficult—and rightfully so. I went along with my friends' desire to stop at the store, even though I dislike Christmas clutter and dislike shopping even more because there was no reason for me to be an inflexible jerk. I paid no price for flexibility in that situation, and my friends enjoyed themselves. I went for a walk later in the day. (Here's a little secret, though. I discovered I don't like girls' weekends. Not my idea of self-care. Adjustments made.)

But Be Assertive Too

On the other end of the spectrum, being too flexible won't work either. Self-care also requires speaking up to make sure that your self-care plan actually delivers the replenishment it's supposed to deliver, and this is where anxiety can subvert your efforts. If you go out to eat with a friend and the soup is cold or the server mistakenly brings you the wrong dish, staying quiet while you eat cold soup is not self-care. And during the normal course of your normal days, you must practice politely speaking up for yourself. If your coworker opens the window and you're freezing but say nothing (or say you're fine when you're actually freezing), that's not self-care. If you are shy and hesitant to speak up, one of the most important patterns to interrupt is *denying your own discomfort.*

A few years ago, I decided to get a pedicure. It's not something I normally do, so it felt a little indulgent. *Good for me*, I thought. *Indulge!* It started off fine. The young man was friendly and said nothing about the horrible condition of my feet. But as he was working, the metal file slipped under my toenail and sliced me, drawing blood. I winced and jumped, he apologized, and we carried on. But he continued to be a bit rough. I tensed my feet, and he repeatedly told me to relax. I said nothing.

And then he took a file to my heel and Achilles tendon, ripping my skin. I started to bleed. He apologized. I nodded and again I said nothing. *Why aren't you saying anything?* I asked myself. I was observing my lack of assertiveness with disdain. *You are a grown-up. An idiot.* He finished the pedicure. I paid, left a generous tip (I *know*!), and went home. My heel became infected. I still call myself an idiot when I think about it, and I still wonder why I allowed that. I think it's that I didn't want to be rude, but believing that my only two options were to be rude or to tolerate the pain (and then get an infection) was a mistake.

Being assertive does not mean that you disregard others. It does not mean you are entitled. But women in particular often feel that they must sacrifice assertiveness to protect relationships. In their book *Women Don't Ask*, authors Linda Babcock and Sara Laschever explore what gets in the way of women negotiating in both business and their personal lives. Their research reveals, not surprisingly, that *women don't ask.* "The impulse to pay attention to relationships is so deeply embedded in women's psyches that they rarely see any of their interactions as *not* having a relationship dimension," they write. Women thus avoid negotiations and asking for what they need or want because they fear damaging the relationship. Babcock and Laschever see this as a false dilemma, a limiting of possible options. "Instead, women need to acknowledge that they almost always have dual goals in a negotiation—issue-related goals and relationship goals—and that they need ways to achieve both."

I haven't had a pedicure since my heel infection. I think I will schedule one, an opportunity to practice some assertive self-care. I, like you, am a work in progress.

And Finally—Uncovering and Adjusting the Seven Patterns Becomes Self-Care

Congratulations. You've audited yourself. You now know how your sneaky anxious patterns operate. You have moved them out of hiding and into the light. And please know this: all the patterns I've described are normal and common. Every single one. Acknowledging these patterns and working to shift them become the best overall self-care solution, the road map to better responses when anxiety and stress show up, which they will. But you are no longer going to do the emotional equivalent of covering your ears, closing your eyes, and singing "La-la-la" as loudly as you can. Anxiety left unrecognized, unchecked, and unexposed gets in the way. No more.

There is no finish line or being done; managing your emotional and social self is about maintenance, a consistent resetting and rebooting. Step forward. Adjust. You are practicing self-care every time you do the following:

- Create a bit of space between you and your worry by externalizing it (pulling it out and giving it a name) and then sharing this approach with those you love.
- Practice unhooking in the moment from your repetitive negative thinking by allowing those thoughts to show up, acknowledging the habit, and then shifting your attention to something interesting outside—something external to your internal dialogue, such as a mountain, a pet, or a group activity.
- Value the different parts of you and others, while moving out of global, all-or-nothing reactions.
- Spend time with others you enjoy and also appreciate your own company, choosing solitude when it suits you.
- Minimize multitasking and move out of the trap of always needing to be busy, productive, and goal-oriented.
- Do something playful and fun. Yes, *fun*.
- Recognize simmering, constant irritability, as a sign that you're stuck in some of your negative patterns, inside and out. Small adjustments matter, so make some.

Above all else, here at the end, I encourage you to share the wonderful, messy, vulnerable parts of yourself. This will not always go well. Anxiety, with its demand for certainty and comfort, will not be pleased. Let's accept together the constant, predictable hum of anxiety's dissatisfaction and still choose to step in: to revel in the adventures and joys that show up when we roll around in the mights and maybes of life.

Simplify, demystify, connect.

QUESTIONS FOR PONDERING AND JOURNALING
How are you doing with the basics of self-care versus self-medication, including sleep, screen time, activity, and substance use?
Are there any ways that your lack of self-care impacts those around you? How about self-medication?
What social/cultural messages do you notice about self-medication?
What feelings or emotions are you most likely to avoid and how do you go about doing that?
What aspects of your self-care do you feel most proud of? Any small adjustments to be made?
Of the seven sneaky patterns of anxiety I described, which do you now recognize as the most powerful for you?

NOTES

CHAPTER 1

pg 13 researcher Susan Nolen-Hoeksema: This is a good summary of Dr. Nolen-Hoeksema's research on rumination and RNT: Lyubomirsky, S., Layous, K., Chancellor, J., & Katherine Nelson, S. (2015). Thinking about rumination: The scholarly contributions and intellectual legacy of Susan Nolen-Hoeksema. *Annual Review of Clinical Psychology, 11*: 1–22. http://sonjalyubomirsky.com/files/2012/09/Lyubomirsky-Layous-Chancellor-Nelson-2015.pdf

Other resources on ruminating and RNT:

Lyubomirsky, S., and Nolen-Hoeksema, S. (1995). Effects of self-focused rumination on negative thinking and interpersonal problem solving. *Journal of Personality and Social Psychology, 69*(1): 176–190. http://sonjalyubomirsky.com/wp-content/themes/sonjalyubomirsky/papers/LN1995.pdf

Monteregge, S., Tsagkalidou, A., Cuijpers, P., & Spinhoven, P. (2020). The effects of different types of treatment for anxiety on repetitive negative thinking: A meta-analysis. *Clinical Psychology: Science and Practice, 27*(2), e12316. https://doi.org/10.1111/cpsp.12316

Nolen-Hoeksema, S. (1991). Responses to depression and their effects on the duration of depressive episodes. *Journal of Abnormal Psychology, 100*(4): 569–582. https://doi.org/10.1037/0021-843X.100.4.569

pg 15 Anxious parents are six to seven times more likely: Ginsburg, G. S. (2009). The Child Anxiety Prevention Study: Intervention model and primary outcomes. *Journal of Consulting and Clinical Psychology, 77*(3): 580–587. https://www.ncbi.nlm.nih.gov/pmc/articles/PMC3373966/

Also see *Anxious Kids, Anxious Parents*, my book coauthored with Reid Wilson, detailing the impact of parental anxiety on children and how to interrupt those patterns.

pg 26 visualization changes the connections and pathways in our brains: For more on the role of neuroplasticity in brains, excellent books include *The Brain That Changes Itself* and *The Brain's Way of Healing* by Norman Doidge.

Interesting research on reduction of pain after surgery using guided imagery interventions on preoperative anxiety and postoperative pain is here:

Àlvarez-García, C., & Yaban, Züleyha Śimśek. (2020). The effects of preoperative guided imagery interventions on preoperative anxiety and postoperative pain: A meta-analysis. *Complementary Therapies in Clinical Practice, 38* (February): 10177. https://www.sciencedirect.com/science/article/pii/S174438811930581X

And athletic performance here:

Ranganathan, V. K., Siemionow, V., Liu, J. Z., Sahgal, V., & Yue, G. H.

(2004). From mental power to muscle power—gaining strength by using the mind. *Neuropsychologia, 42*(7): 944–956. https://pubmed.ncbi.nlm.nih.gov/14998709/

pg 29 CBT-i Coach app: US Department of Veterans Affairs, VA Mobile, BCT-I Coach. https://mobile.va.gov/app/cbt-i-coach

CHAPTER 2

pg 41 The Pain Catastrophizing Scale (PCS): Leung L. (2012). Pain catastrophizing: An updated review. *Indian Journal of Psychological Medicine, 34*(3): 204–217. https://doi.org/10.4103/0253-7176.106012

Sullivan, M. J. L., Bishop, S. R., & Pivik, J. (1995). The Pain Catastrophizing Scale: Development and validation. *Psychological Assessment, 7*(4): 524–532. https://doi.org/10.1037/1040-3590.7.4.524

pg 42 people going into surgery: Baxter, J. et al. (2016). The role of psychosocial factors in the pain experience: The relationship between depression, catastrophizing and chronic pain. *Journal of Pain, 17*(4): S97–S98. https://doi.org/10.1016/j.jpain.2016.01.299

pg 42 a single question assessing catastrophic pain: Lutz, J., Gross, R., Long, D., & Cox, S. (2017). Predicting risk for opioid use in chronic pain with a single-item measure of catastrophic thinking. *Journal of the American Board of Family Medicine, 30*(6): 828–831. https://www.jabfm.org/content/jabfp/30/6/828.full.pdf

pg 42 parental catastrophizing about a child's pain: Goubert, L., & Simons, L. E. (2013). Cognitive styles and processes in paediatric pain. In *Oxford Textbook of Paediatric Pain*, ed., P. J. McGrath, B. J. Stevens, S. M. Walker, and W. T. Zempsky, 95–101. Oxford: Oxford University Press.

Caes, L., van Gampelaere, C., Van Hoecke, E., Van Winckel, M., Kamoen, K., & Goubert, L. (2021). Parental catastrophizing and goal pursuit in the context of child chronic pain: A daily diary study. *Frontiers in Psychology* 12:680546.

pg 46 many insomniacs are rather lousy at gauging: Harvey, A., & Tang, N. (2012, January). (Mis)perception of sleep in insomnia: A puzzle and a resolution. *Psychological Bulletin Journal, 138*(1): 77–101. https://www.ncbi.nlm.nih.gov/pmc/articles/PMC3277880/pdf/nihms328578.pdf

pg 51 Writer Niedria Dionne Kenny: *Phenomenally Me, My Sweet* 2016, (2016, January 9). CreateSpace Independent Publishing Platform.

pg 59 article about playgrounds: Barry, E. (2018, March 10). In Britain's playgrounds, "bringing in risk" to build resilience. *New York Times.* https://www.nytimes.com/2018/03/10/world/europe/britain-playgrounds-risk.html

CHAPTER 3

pg 66 the effectiveness of many informational programs designed to prevent abduction: Kulkofsky, S. (n.d.) An assessment of the effectiveness of child abduction education, https://www.human.cornell.edu/sites/default/files/HD/circ/Stranger%20danger_Kulkofsky.pdf

pg 71 Trauma expert Lisa Ferentz: Ferentz, L. (2016, September/October). Transcending trauma: Learning how to guide devastated clients toward growth. Psychotherapy Networker. https://www.psychotherapynetworker.org/magazine/article/1039/transcending-trauma

pg 71 concept of post-traumatic growth: Tedeschi, R., & Calhoun, L. (2004, April 1). Posttraumatic growth: A new perspective on psychotraumatology. *Psychiatric Times, 21*(4). https://www.bu.edu/wheelock/

files/2018/05/Article-Tedeschi-and-Lawrence-Calhoun-Posttraumatic-Growth-2014.pdf

CHAPTER 4

pg 85 Esther Perel said it beautifully: Esther Perel: The erotic is an antidote to death. (2019, July 11 [original air date]; 2021, July 8 [last updated]). *On Being with Krista Tippett.* https://onbeing.org/programs/esther-perel-the-erotic-is-an-antidote-to-death/

pg 100 lonely people tend to be more self-focused and less responsive: Jones, W., Hobbs, S., & Hockenbury, D. (1982). Loneliness and social skill deficits. *Journal of Personality and Social Psychology, 42*: 682–669. https://www.researchgate.net/publication/16120577_Loneliness_and_social_skill_deficits

pg 104 social comparison and its contribution to disconnection and loneliness: Peplau, L. A. (1985). Preventing the harmful consequences of severe and persistent loneliness: Proceedings of a research planning workshop held in cooperation with the Department of Health and Human Services, February 10–12, 1982. Washington, DC: US GPO.

pg 105 examining the loneliness and disconnection felt by eighteen- to thirty-four-year-olds: Lisitsa, E., Benjamin, K. S., Chun, S. K., Skalisky, J., Hammond, L. E., & Mezulis, A. H. (2020). Loneliness among young adults during covid-19 pandemic: The mediational roles of social media use and social support seeking. *Journal of Social and Clinical Psychology, 39*(8): 708–726.

pg 106 Society may have told some women: racheljsimmons, Instagram, https://www.instagram.com/p/CWW_B2dsx1f/?utm_medium=Twitter

pg 106 rates of loneliness up to 50 percent higher: CIGNA. (2018). CIGNA U.S. Loneliness Index: Survey of 20,000 Americans examining behaviors driving loneliness in the United States. https://www.multivu.com/players/English/8294451-cigna-us-loneliness-survey/

Achterbergh, L., Pitman, A., Birken, M. et al. (2020). The experience of loneliness among young people with depression: A qualitative meta-synthesis of the literature. *BMC Psychiatry, 20*(415). https://doi.org/10.1186/s12888-020-02818-3

pg 118 As Rachel Simmons: https://www.linkedin.com/posts/rachel-simmons-5333a5152_be-yourself-is-an-oft-dispensed-nugget-activity-6866554215846744064-7Q2o?utm_source=linkedin_share&utm_medium=member_desktop_web

pg 119 interviewed Esther Perel: Esther Perel: The erotic is an antidote to death. (2019, July 11 [original air date]; 2021, July 8 [last updated]). *On Being with Krista Tippett.* https://onbeing.org/programs/esther-perel-the-erotic-is-an-antidote-to-death/

pg 120 Evan Briggs documentary: Briggs, E. (dir.) (2017). *The growing season.* http://thegrowingseasonfilm.com

pg 121 2015 Tedx Talk, Briggs said this: Briggs, E. (2015, December 16). Mixing across generations. TEDxSnoIsleLibraries. https://www.youtube.com/watch?v=5Walt8nPINM

pg 121 the incorporation of volunteer work as a part of treatment for depressed teens: Ballard, P. J., Daniel, S. S., Anderson, G., Nicolotti, L., Caballero Quinones, E., Lee, M., & Koehler, A. N. (2021). Incorporating volunteering into treatment for depression among adolescents: Developmental and clinical considerations. *Frontiers in Psychiatry, 12*: 642910. doi: 10.3389/fpsyg.2021.642910

pg 123 complicated relationship between social media and social support seeking:

Lisitsa, E., Benjamin, K. S., Chun, S. K., Skalisky, J., Hammond, L. E., & Mezulis, A. H. (2020). Loneliness among young adults during covid-19 pandemic: The mediational roles of social media use and social support seeking. *Journal of Social and Clinical Psychology, 39*(8): 708–726.

CHAPTER 5

pg 127 during the height of the lockdown: Miller, C. C. (2020, May 6). Nearly half of men say they do most of the home schooling. 3 percent of women agree. https://www.nytimes.com/2020/05/06/upshot/pandemic-chores-homeschooling-gender.html

pg 129 studied interruptions among office workers: Mark, G., Gudith, D., & Klocke, U. (n.d.) The cost of interrupted work: More speed and stress. UCI Donald Bren School of Information and Computer Sciences. https://www.ics.uci.edu/~gmark/chi08-mark.pdf; Thorne, B. (2020, February 13). How distractions at work take up more time than you think. I Done This Blog. http://blog.idonethis.com/distractions-at-work/

pg 129 impairment similar to driving drunk: Strayer, D. L., Drews, F. A., & Crouch, D. J. (2006, Summer). A comparison of the cell phone driver and the drunk driver. *Human Factors, 48*(2): 381–391. https://pubmed.ncbi.nlm.nih.gov/16884056/

pg 129 "The Myth of Multitasking": Rosen, C. (2008, Spring). The myth of multitasking: How intentional self-distraction hurts us. The New Atlantis. https://www.thenewatlantis.com/publications/the-myth-of-multitasking

pg 130 the creation of such a lifestyle: Silvia Bellezza, Neeru Paharia, Anat Keinan, Conspicuous Consumption of Time: When Busyness and Lack of Leisure Time Become a Status Symbol, *Journal of Consumer Research,* Volume 44, Issue 1, June 2017, Pages 118-138, https://doi.org/10.1093/jcr/ucw076

pg 132 complain the most about work: Robinson, J. R., Martin, S., Glorieux, I., & Minnen, J. (2011, June). The overestimated workweek revisited. *Monthly Labor Review*: 43–53. https://www.bls.gov/opub/mlr/2011/06/art3full.pdf

CHAPTER 6

pg 150 the level of irritability in children: Vidal-Ribas, P., Brotman, M. A., Valdivieso, I., Leibenluft, E. & Stringaris, A. (2016). The status of irritability in psychiatry: A conceptual and quantitative review. *Journal of the American Academy of Adolescent Psychiatry, 55*(7): 556–570. https://www.ncbi.nlm.nih.gov/pmc/articles/PMC4927461/pdf/main.pdf

pg 151 "Irritability" is defined as: Bell, E., Bryant, R., Boyce, P., Porter, R., & Malhi, G. (2021). Irritability through research domain criteria: An opportunity for transdiagnostic conceptualisation. *BJPsych Open, 7*(1): E36. doi:10.1192/bjo.2020.168

CHAPTER 7

pg 168 phone use before bed: Technology Networks: Neuroscience and Research News. (2021, April 27). Can blue light filters really help you sleep better? https://www.technologynetworks.com/neuroscience/news/can-blue-light-filters-really-help-your-sleep-better-348176

pg 168 sleep deprivation and screens: Hale, L., Kirschen, G. W., LeBourgeois, M. K., Gradisar, M., Garrison, M. M., Montgomery-Downs, H., Kirschen, H., McHale, S. M., Chang, A. M., & Buxton, O. M. (2018). Youth screen media habits and sleep: Sleep-friendly screen behavior recommendations for clinicians, educators, and parents. *Child and adolescent psychiatric clinics of North America, 27*(2): 229–245. https://www.ncbi.nlm.nih.gov/pmc/articles/PMC5839336/

pg 169 one night of sleep deprivation: Harrison, Y., & Horne, J. A. (1999). One night of sleep loss impairs innovative thinking and flexible decision making. *Organizational Behavior and Human Decision Processes, 78*(2): 128–145.

pg 171 increased in women by 84 percent: Peltier, M. R., Verplaetse, T. L., Mineur, Y. S., Petrakis, I. L., Cosgrove, K. P., Picciotto, M. R., & McKee, S. A. (2019). Sex differences in stress-related alcohol use. *Neurobiology of Stress, 10*: 100149. https://doi.org/10.1016/j.ynstr.2019.100149

pg 171 substantive increase in female drinking: Pollard, M. S., Tucker, J. S., & Green, H. D. (2020, September). Changes in adult alcohol use and consequences during the covid-19 pandemic in the US. *JAMA Network Open, 3*(9): doi: 10.1001/jamanetworkopen.2020.22942

pg 172 using alcohol to self-medicate: Turner, S., Mota, N., Bolton, J., & Sareen, J. (2018). Self-medication with alcohol or drugs for mood and anxiety disorders: A narrative review of the epidemiological literature. *Depression and Anxiety, 35*(9): 851–860. https://doi.org/10.1002/da.22771

pg 172 alcohol impairs your ability to stay asleep: Stein, M. D., & Friedmann, P. D. (2005). Disturbed sleep and its relationship to alcohol use. *Substance Abuse, 26*(1): 1–13. https://doi.org/10.1300/j465v26n01_01

pg 174 content in marijuana plants was 17 to 28 percent: Stuyt, E. (2018). The problem with the current high-potency THC marijuana from the perspective of an addiction psychiatrist. *Missouri Medicine, 115*(6): 482–486.

pg 174 A study done in Australia: Patton, G. C., Coffey, C., Carlin, J. B., Degenhardt, L., Lynskey, M., & Hall, W. (2002). Cannabis use and mental health in young people: Cohort study. *British Medical Journal (Clinical Research Ed.), 325*(7374): 1195–1198. https://doi.org/10.1136/bmj.325.7374.1195

pg 174 how and when to use cannabis to treat anxiety: Sharpe, L., Sinclair, J., Kramer, A., et al. (2020). Cannabis, a cause for anxiety? A critical appraisal of the anxiogenic and anxiolytic properties. *Journal of Translational Medicine, 18*(374): https://rdcu.be/cJVtq

pg 175 the flaw in this thinking: Lembke, A. (2021). *Dopamine nation: Finding balance in the age of indulgence.* New York: Dutton.

pg 176 taking benzodiazepines for anxiety: Tanguay Bernard, M. M., Luc, M., Carrier, J. D., Fournier, L., Duhoux, A., Côté, E., Lessard, O., Gibeault, C., Bocti, C., & Roberge, P. (2018). Patterns of benzodiazepines use in primary care adults with anxiety disorders. *Heliyon, 4*(7), e00688. https://doi.org/10.1016/j.heliyon.2018.e00688

Lader, M. (2011, December). Benzodiazepines revisited—will we ever learn? *Addiction* (Abingdon, UK), *106*(12): 2086–2109. https://doi.org/10.1111/j.1360-0443.2011.03563.x

pg 177 an informational July 2021 webinar: Public workshop: Safe use of benzodiazepines: Clinical, regulatory, and public health perspectives. (2021, July 12–13). Duke University Margolis Center for Health Policy. https://healthpolicy.duke.edu/events/safe-use-benzodiazepines-clinical-regulatory-and-public-health-perspectives

pg 177 stronger black-box warning: FDA requiring Boxed Warning updated to improved safe use of benzodiazepine drug class. (2022, January 14 [latest current content]). https://www.fda.gov/drugs/fda-drug-safety-podcasts/fda-requiring-boxed-warning-updated-improve-safe-use-benzodiazepine-drug-class

pg 179 Swedish study followed almost 400,000 cross-country skiers: Svensson, M., Brundin, L., Erhardt, S., Hållmarker, U., James, S., & Deierborg, T. (2021, September 10). Physical activity is associated with lower long-term incidence of anxiety in a population-based, large-scale study. *Frontiers in Psychiatry, 12*: 714014. doi: 10.3389/fpsyt.2021.714014

pg 183 sacrifice assertiveness to protect relationships: Babcock, L., & Laschever, S. (2003). *Women don't ask: Negotiation and the gender divide*. Princeton, NJ: Princeton University Press.

ACKNOWLEDGMENTS

When I wrote my last book, my boys were teenagers. They and my husband tolerated the piles of paper and books on the kitchen island and the hours I spent working, somehow finding a way to be wonderfully present and respectfully unobtrusive at the same time. For this book, the pandemic brought them home again, like it or not, to witness another project, this time as even more delightful young men. To my husband Crawford and my sons Brackett and Zed, I thank you for the laughter and love you gave me during this book and always. How lucky I am that you were—and are—here.

My parents Cathleen and Ed Gerwig are constant voices of encouragement, and I cherish them more than words can express. Their childhoods were filled with challenges, yet as they celebrate sixty years of marriage this year, they have worked consciously to change the course, showing their children and grandchildren how to create a family built on connection, commitment, and love.

I am lucky to have my siblings Nancy, Ed, and Robin in my corner. They are my funny, wonderful friends and I just love them. Their kids are equally wonderful. The Greens complete the clan. We are a family full of laughter and flaws, with plenty of both to go around.

Robin is also my intrepid Flusterclux podcasting partner. It was her idea to start a podcast and to create the original Anxiety Audit course during the height of the pandemic. She encouraged me to expand the course into a book. I am in constant awe of her capacity to take ideas and make them happen.

Michael Yapko is a generous, brilliant, and ever-supportive mentor and friend. For over thirty years he has taught me how to define a problem and communicate solutions. The importance of asking HOW questions and the focus on recognizing and teaching important skills come directly from Michael. He has made an enormous difference in my life, and I am deeply grateful.

Fifteen years ago, Reid Wilson asked me to write a book with him. I ended up with much more than I thought possible: two books, not one, and an enduring connection I treasure. I have learned so much from Reid professionally. Personally, our friendship means the world to me.

I have wonderful "therapist" friends and many of them contributed to this book through their own brilliant words, conversations, and support. Thank you to Michele Weiner-Davis, Rick Miller, Jay Essif, Rachel Simmons, Lisa Ferentz, and Jeffrey Zeig.

Christine Cook continues to define what friendship should be. And she lives down the street. I hope you all have a Christine in your lives. Karen Shepard has been my dear friend for almost forty years. I adore her. She's a real writer—the brilliant kind, so when she told me I could get this book finished, I believed her. Such is the power of four decades of Karen cheering you on, laughing at your jokes, and showing you how it's done.

Thank you to Allison Janse, Christian Blonshine, and the entire

Health Communications, Inc. team for helping me bring this book to life and for our years of partnership.

And as always, I am appreciative of the families that share their stories with me and listen to mine. The details of stories I share in this book have been changed to protect privacy, but the struggles, the emotions, the connections, and the victories are real, and mean so much to me.

ABOUT THE AUTHOR

Lynn Lyons, LICSW, is a psychotherapist specializing in the treatment of anxiety in adults and children. She has been in private practice for thirty years and travels extensively as a speaker and trainer on the subject of anxiety, its role in families, and the need for a preventative approach at home and in schools.

With a special interest in breaking the generational cycle of worry in families, she is the author of several books and articles on anxiety, including with co-author Reid Wilson, *Anxious Kids, Anxious Parents: 7 Ways to Stop the Worry Cycle and Raise Courageous & Independent Children* and the companion book for kids, *Playing with Anxiety: Casey's Guide for Teens and Kids,* and the award-winning text *Using Hypnosis with Children: Creating and Delivering Effective Interventions.*

Lynn is the co-host of the popular podcast Flusterclux with her sister-in-law Robin Hutson. She is a sought-after expert, being interviewed for her insights in the *New York Times, Time, NPR, Psychology Today, The Atlantic,* and other media outlets.

Lynn lives in her New Hampshire home with her husband where she hikes, bikes, and walks whenever she can. Her two sons returned to the nest during the pandemic but are now out finding their way in the world.

NOTES

NOTES

NOTES